Esty

How to Become an Esty Seller and Money Making Techniques

(Definitive Guides for Future Online Business Strategies and Converting Website)

Kenneth Merritt

Published By **Oliver Leish**

Kenneth Merritt

All Rights Reserved

Esty: How to Become an Esty Seller and Money Making Techniques (Definitive Guides for Future Online Business Strategies and Converting Website)

ISBN 978-1-7771142-3-7

No part of this guidebook shall be reproduced in any form without permission in writing from the publisher except in the case of brief quotations embodied in critical articles or reviews.

Legal & Disclaimer

The information contained in this book is not designed to replace or take the place of any form of medicine or professional medical advice. The information in this book has been provided for educational & entertainment purposes only.

The information contained in this book has been compiled from sources deemed reliable, and it is accurate to the best of the Author's knowledge; however, the Author cannot guarantee its accuracy and validity and cannot be held liable for any errors or omissions. Changes are periodically made to this book. You must consult your doctor or get professional medical advice before using any of the suggested remedies, techniques, or information in this book.

Upon using the information contained in this book, you agree to hold harmless the Author from and against any damages, costs, and expenses, including any legal fees potentially resulting from the application of any of the information provided by this guide. This disclaimer applies to any damages or injury caused by the use and application, whether directly or indirectly, of any advice or information presented, whether for breach of contract, tort, negligence, personal injury, criminal intent, or under any other cause of action.

You agree to accept all risks of using the information presented inside this book. You need to consult a professional medical practitioner in order to ensure you are both able and healthy enough to participate in this program.

Table Of Contents

Chapter 1: The Stage For Etsy Success 1

Chapter 2: Crafting Irresistible Products 26

Chapter 3: Mastering Etsy Shop Setup ... 52

Chapter 4: Marketing Your Etsy Shop 79

Chapter 5: Delivering Exceptional Customer Service 108

Chapter 6: What To Sell 132

Chapter 7: Setting Up Your Shop 151

Chapter 1: The Stage For Etsy Success

Subsection 1: Welcome to the Etsy Ecosystem.

As I took my first steps into the enchanting worldwide of Etsy, I could not assist however feel a hurry of excitement. It modified into like stepping into a bustling artisan bazaar, teeming with creativity and entrepreneurial spirit. Etsy isn't always virtually a web market; it is a colourful environment wherein dreams are woven into the very fabric of its existence.

Overview of Etsy's Unique Marketplace.

Picture this: a web platform wherein over 4 million revolutionary entrepreneurs from round the arena accumulate to expose off their craftsmanship. This is Etsy. It's a mystical marketplace in which the normal turns into incredible. Here, artisans, artists, and craftsmen come collectively to offer home made and unique products that cross past the heavily produced, cookie-cutter worldwide we often discover ourselves in.

Etsy is not pretty plenty selling merchandise; it's about telling tales via your creations. It's in which the attraction of a hand-knit scarf, the beauty of a hand-painted vase, or the individuality of a customised necklace takes middle degree. In a global in which hundreds feels automatic, Etsy is a sanctuary for the individual touch.

Imagine your self as an Etsy dealer. You're no longer sincerely peddling wares; you are crafting a narrative. Your shop will become a degree, and every product is someone with its personal story. And that is wherein the magic takes area - the stories you tell through your creations connect with people on a deeply emotional diploma. They're no longer genuinely searching for a product; they're investing to your passion and artistry.

The Potential for Success on Etsy.

Etsy is not top notch a platform for progressive expression, but it is also a springboard for achievement. The capacity proper right here is boundless. In the substantial ocean of e-trade, Etsy is like a cushty pond wherein small fish can thrive and develop into robust leviathans.

Consider the tale of Sarah, a photograph fashion designer who decided to show her hand-lettering interest right right into a commercial corporation. She opened her Etsy keep, "InkSplendid," and inner a year, her custom bridal ceremony invitation designs have turn out to be wildly famous. Sarah's annual income skyrocketed, permitting her to go away her 9-to-five approach and reputation on her proper ardour complete-time. That's the kind of success Etsy can offer.

But fulfillment on Etsy isn't always restrained to a pick out few. It's democratic. It's about your creativity, your willpower, and your capability to conform and take a look at. Whether you are a pro artisan or a budding entrepreneur, there's an area for you right right here.

Inspiring Success Stories.

Let me introduce you to Maria, a unmarried mom who grew to emerge as her love for knitting proper proper right into a thriving Etsy organisation referred to as "CozyKnits." With now not whatever but a few knitting needles and a whole lot of power of will, Maria started out small. Her first sale have turn out to be a modest beanie. But Maria did not surrender. She honed her craft, improved her product snap shots, and listened to consumer feedback. Today, she ships her comfortable creations international, assisting her circle of relatives even as doing what she loves.

Then there is Michael, a retired teacher who located his second calling making custom timber toys. His Etsy save, "WoodenWonders," started as a hobby, however it quick changed right into a deliver of pride and income. His toys, hand made with love and precision, have determined their way into homes at a few degree inside the globe.

These memories are not outliers. They're just a glimpse of what's possible on Etsy. The platform is a degree playing problem where your creativity, tough art work, and passion can propel you to success beyond your wildest dreams.

So, welcome to Etsy, wherein creativity is aware of no bounds, success is internal reach, and idea flows like a river. This is your degree, your tale, and your possibility to shine. Buckle up, due to the fact we are about to embark on a adventure that would alternate your existence and make your goals a reality.

Subsection 2: Crafting Your Vision.

Choosing Your Niche and Product Line.

As I released into my Etsy journey, one of the maximum crucial steps I took end up selecting the right place of interest and product line. This selection gadgets the tone on your complete Etsy challenge. Here's how I approached it:

Discover Your Passion: The first actual trouble I did turned into soul-searching. I requested myself, "What am I in reality captivated with?" Etsy is all approximately creativity and particular merchandise, so choosing a spot you simply care about is important. For example, if you're a die-difficult vintage fanatic or an eco-conscious crafter, permit that passion guide your desire.

Market Research: Once I had a few thoughts brewing, I delved into marketplace studies. Etsy has a treasure trove of information and system that will help you with this. I scoured Etsy's are trying to find bar to find famous merchandise in my functionality niches, being attentive to the quantity of listings and their expenses. This gave me insights into what became in name for and what wasn't.

Assess Your Skills: Remember that your Etsy hold ought to showcase your information. So, I assessed my talents and skills. If you are an splendid earrings maker, probable it surely is your location of interest. If you're professional at virtual artwork, find out that road. Your product line have to align in conjunction with your skills.

Unique Angle: Consider what specific mindset or twist you could deliver to your preferred location of hobby. Let's say you make a decision to create hand-painted tote baggage. Can you infuse your love for natural worldwide into your designs, making them stand proud of the rest? Finding that particular perspective may be a recreation-changer.

Longevity: Think approximately the lengthy-term ability of your area of interest. Is it a passing style, or does it have staying power? Trends may be profitable, but they can also fizzle out fast. I opted for a gap with enduring enchantment to make sure the sturdiness of my Etsy store.

Identifying Your Target Audience.

Now which you've nailed down your region of interest and product line, it is time to understand your target market. Knowing who you're developing for will make your advertising efforts extra effective and your products more appealing.

Create Customer Personas: Start through crafting purchaser personas. These are fictional representations of your high-quality customers. Give them names, a long time, and interests. What troubles can your merchandise solve for them? For instance, if you're promoting handcrafted child clothes, your character might be "Sarah, a trendy mother in her 30s, who values sustainable and cute apparel for her toddler."

Market Segmentation: Divide your capability clients into segments based totally totally totally on shared characteristics. These is probably demographics like age, gender, region, or psychographics like pursuits and way of life. Segmenting allows you tailor your advertising messages to unique groups.

Competitor Analysis: Look at successful Etsy shops on your place of hobby. Who are their clients? What do their reviews show about the customers? This research can offer precious insights into the varieties of customers your keep may also attract.

Solve Problems: Consider how your merchandise can remedy your goal marketplace's problems or meet their dreams. When you apprehend what troubles your clients face, you could deal with them right away in your product listings and advertising.

Setting Achievable Goals.

With your vicinity of interest and intention market in thoughts, it's time to set a few capability dreams. Goal-placing is like charting your direction in this Etsy journey.

SMART Goals: I'm certain you've got heard of SMART dreams – Specific, Measurable, Achievable, Relevant, and Time-advantageous. Apply this framework in your Etsy desires. For example, "I will collect one hundred income in my first six months on Etsy with the useful resource of constantly list 3 new products each week and attractive with customers every day."

Start Small: While it is high-quality to have large goals, starting small will let you bring together momentum. Begin with possible short-term goals, like engaging in your first 10 income, and then paintings your manner as much as greater ambitious targets.

Flexibility: Etsy can be unpredictable, so be prepared to conform your dreams as wanted. If a specific product isn't always promoting as expected, be open to pivoting or refining your approach.

Track Your Progress: Use equipment inside Etsy and outside software to tune your improvement. Regularly evaluation your dreams and alter your strategies therefore.

Crafting your imaginative and prescient on your Etsy maintain is a thrilling device. It's the inspiration upon which you will construct your business. Take some time, do your research, and infuse your passion into every detail. Your adventure on Etsy has certainly all started out, and the possibilities are limitless.

Subsection 3: Legal and Financial Foundations.

Welcome to the interesting international of Etsy entrepreneurship! I'm right here to manual you through the nitty-gritty of criminal and economic foundations a excellent manner to lay the strong basis for your Etsy fulfillment. In this monetary damage, we are diving into the critical components of registering your shop and industrial corporation, unraveling the mysteries of taxes and monetary making plans, and uncovering pricing strategies in an effort to have your profit margins soaring.

Registering Your Shop and Business.

Before you can start raking inside the ones Etsy dollars, you may need to make matters actual. Registering your hold and business organisation is greater than truely bureaucratic workplace work; it's miles approximately organising your logo's legitimacy and safeguarding your future.

Think of your shop call because the flag that alerts your presence in Etsy's bustling marketplace. It's your identity, so select out it efficaciously. Remember, it must resonate collectively with your merchandise and be memorable to capacity clients. Once you have got settled on a call that sings to your soul, head to Etsy's easy-to-comply with registration device. This is wherein you can add all of the ones crucial hold records - your logo, banner, save regulations, and a captivating 'About' segment.

But do not prevent there. For legal features, it is important to keep in mind your business organization form. Will you use as a sole proprietor, LLC, or employer? Each has its professionals and cons, like crook responsibility and taxation implications. Consulting with a prison expert or accountant can be a recreation-changer right here, ensuring you choose out the proper shape to shield your private home and reduce tax burdens.

Understanding Taxes and Financial Planning.

Ah, taxes—the ever-looming cloud on every entrepreneur's horizon. Fear not; we are in this together. Etsy does a awesome task of helping you bought sales tax from buyers, but it's miles critical to recognize the nuances.

Sales tax fees range with the aid of location, and some states don't have any profits tax in any respect. To make certain you're charging the appropriate quantity, you'll possibly need to do a bit of research or are searching for advice from a tax professional. Failing to acquire the right amount may additionally need to bring about results or headaches down the street.

On the flip side, remember approximately your profits tax duties. Depending to your business shape, you could either report your Etsy profits on your non-public tax return or file a separate industrial employer go back. Keeping meticulous facts of your income and prices is a want to. There are masses of person-great accounting software program software alternatives available, like QuickBooks or Xero, to help you stay prepared.

Pricing Strategies for Profit.

Now, permit's get all the manner all of the manner all the way down to the nuts and bolts of pricing your products. This is not a guessing enterprise; it's miles a strategic dance. You need to make coins, however you furthermore mght want to be competitive. Finding that sweet spot can be hard, however it's far oh-so-profitable.

Start by way of way of calculating your production expenses. This includes materials, difficult work, and any overhead charges like shipping and Etsy expenses. Once you have got crunched the ones numbers, you can determine to your profits margin. Remember, it is not quite tons masking fees; it's far about building a sustainable commercial business enterprise.

Competitor research is your mystery weapon. See what similar merchandise are promoting for and aim to place your self competitively. If your devices provide precise functions or superior awesome, don't hesitate to rate a top fee. And do no longer be afraid to modify your prices over time as your business enterprise evolves or your fees exchange.

One pricing approach to bear in mind is fee-delivered pricing. This manner packaging your products with fee-boosting extras, like wonderful customer support, precise packaging, or informative product descriptions. These added touches can justify barely higher fees and enhance your consumer's normal enjoy.

In a nutshell, laying your criminal and financial foundations does not need to be daunting. Register your shop with care, get comfy with tax basics, and draw close the artwork of pricing for income. With those requirements for your arsenal, you are properly in your way to Etsy stardom. Stay tuned for the subsequent financial disaster, where we're going to dive deep into crafting impossible to face up to products that clients can't resist!

Subsection 4: Building a Strong Brand.

As you embark on this journey to begin your a hit Etsy shop, one of the maximum crucial factors to bear in thoughts is building a strong brand. In this subsection, I'm going to stroll you thru the artwork of crafting a memorable keep call, crafting a compelling store story, and designing a standout brand and banner that allows you to set your store apart from the crowd.

Creating a Memorable Shop Name.

Think of your keep name because of the reality the number one have an effect on you're making on potential clients. It's like a virtual storefront signal that ought to pique interest and stick in humans's minds. Here are some guidelines to help you create a memorable save call:

1. Reflect Your Niche: Your preserve call have to supply functionality clients a touch about what you promote. If you reflect onconsideration on domestic made rings, as an instance, hold in mind incorporating words like "gems," "craft," or "artisan" into your call.

2. Keep It Short and Sweet: Shorter names are less complex to hold in mind and kind. Aim for a call it certainly is easy to spell and pronounce.

3. Unique and Unforgettable: Check if the call you have got were given in thoughts is already in use on Etsy. You need to keep away from confusion with one-of-a-kind shops. Also, ensure it is not trademarked via someone else.

four. Avoid Trends: While it is tempting to leap at the current style, don't forget the durability of your maintain name. Will it nonetheless make feel and be relevant in some years?

5. Test It Out: Share your capability maintain name with pals and family to get their feedback. Does it resonate with them? Is it catchy?

Crafting a Compelling Shop Story.

Now which you have a awesome preserve name, allow's paintings to your save's story. Your store story is your possibility to connect to customers on a personal diploma. It's a hazard to tell them why you do what you do and what makes your merchandise precise.

1. Share Your Passion: Start with the aid of the use of explaining why you are enthusiastic about your craft. What drives you to create the ones particular gadgets? Customers like to help artisans who certainly love what they do.

2. Tell Your Journey: Share the story of the manner your maintain came to be. Did you begin making jewelry as a interest after

which determined to show it into a business organization? People like to pay interest approximately non-public trips.

3. Highlight Your Values: If you have got got a dedication to sustainability, moral sourcing, or one-of-a-kind values, make certain to say them. This can resonate with clients who percentage your values.

four. Engage Emotionally: Use emotional language and storytelling strategies to engage your target marketplace. Paint a photo of what it is like to very private really certainly one of your merchandise.

Designing a Standout Logo and Banner.

Visuals depend inside the international of online shopping, and your emblem and banner are the visible identification of your logo. Here's a manner to motive them to stand out:

1. Consistency is Key: Your brand and banner ought to be ordinary collectively with your hold's name and story. Use the identical

sunglasses, fonts, and style factors to create a cohesive look.

2. Simplicity Sells: Keep your brand easy and without trouble recognizable. It must look particular in each small and big sizes. Think about how it will appear on product labels and packaging.

3. Professionalism Counts: If you're now not a layout whiz, recall hiring a expert photo clothier. They will let you create a logo and banner that look polished and attractive.

four. Banner as a Showcase: Your banner is high real assets to show off your merchandise or deliver your brand's individual. Use first rate pix that represent your craft.

five. Stay on Brand: Make nice your brand and banner reflect the essence of your emblem. If you sell antique gadgets, a retro-inspired format may fit incredible, while a current, minimalist appearance need to in form handmade candles.

Remember, your store call, maintain story, logo, and banner are all necessary elements of your logo's identification. Take the time to get them proper, and you may be nicely in your way to Etsy fulfillment. Your emblem is what units you aside, makes you memorable, and draws clients in your digital storefront. So, get innovative, and allow your brand shine!

Subsection 5: Sourcing and Supplies.

Ah, sourcing and property - it's miles the backbone of your Etsy undertaking, and it is able to every make or break your keep's achievement. As you embark for your adventure to Etsy stardom, those are the elements on the way to set you apart from the competition and make sure you're constructing a sustainable commercial company. Let's dive deep into the arena of sourcing, inventory manipulate, and green practices.

Finding Reliable Suppliers and Materials.

When I started out my Etsy maintain, I scoured the internet, close by markets, and trade shows to find out companies who matched my vision. It's critical to installation relationships with reliable carriers who can provide you with constant, incredible materials. Here's how:

1. Do Your Homework: Research capability providers very well. Read opinions, ask for samples, and determine their reliability. Don't rush this step; it's miles the muse of your industrial organisation.

2. Network Within Your Niche: Attend business agency occasions and connect to fellow Etsy dealers. They ought to probable in truth share their relied on corporations with you. This form of insider facts can be 24-karat gold.

3. Negotiate Wisely: Negotiating fees and terms with providers is an paintings. Be respectful but business enterprise, and do no longer be afraid to are looking for better

offers, specially as your commercial enterprise company grows.

Managing Inventory Effectively.

Now, permit's talk about inventory. It's clean to get carried away and overstock your merchandise, tying up your precious capital. Here's a way to keep your inventory in take a look at:

1. Track Your Sales: Use Etsy's integrated tools or 1/three-celebration software application software to show your profits tendencies. Knowing what's promoting and what isn't, assist you to inventory up on the proper products on the proper time.

2. Set Reorder Points: Determine at what stock stage you need to reorder substances. This continues your production flowing without problems with out overstocking.

three. Implement the FIFO Method: FIFO, or "First In, First Out," method selling your oldest stock first. This prevents substances from sitting round too prolonged and ensures product freshness.

Tips for Sustainable and Eco-Friendly Sourcing.

In this age of conscious consumerism, embracing sustainable and green sourcing practices may be a activity-changer for your Etsy keep. Not great is it relevant for the planet, however it can additionally lure a faithful patron base who values environmentally responsible groups. Here's a manner to move inexperienced:

1. Choose Eco-Friendly Materials: Opt for substances which might be renewable, recycled, or biodegradable. Bamboo, natural cotton, and recycled metals are only some examples.

2. Local Sourcing: Whenever viable, guide close by artisans and companies. Not only does this reduce your carbon footprint, however it moreover strengthens your network ties.

3. Reduce, Reuse, Recycle: Get revolutionary along aspect your sourcing through upcycling materials or repurposing vintage devices. This no longer only gives strong point to your merchandise however moreover reduces waste.

Putting It All Together.

As you mission into the arena of Etsy, consider that sourcing and belongings are the constructing blocks of your achievement. Finding reliable vendors, dealing with stock accurately, and embracing sustainable practices can set you at the path to Etsy greatness. It's a adventure, and every so often you could stumble, but with perseverance and those savvy sourcing techniques, your Etsy store will thrive proper away. Happy crafting!

Chapter 2: Crafting Irresistible Products

Subsection 1: Product Development Essentials.

Hello there, aspiring Etsy entrepreneur! In this thrilling chapter, we're diving deep into the very essence of your Etsy store's achievement: crafting not possible to withstand products. Whether you're absolutely beginning or already a seasoned supplier looking for to up your hobby, reading the ones product improvement requirements is fundamental to prevailing over customers and maintaining them coming over again for added.

Choosing the Right Materials.

Picture this: You've determined to open a store selling home made earrings. You have your designs sketched out, your preserve call picked, but now it's time to hold your creations to existence. This is wherein your cloth alternatives come into play.

Imagine you want to create stylish, green rings. In this situation, you will want to discover sustainable substances like recycled metals or natural gemstones. These picks no longer best align along side your emblem's values however moreover resonate with a growing sizable fashion of environmentally conscious clients.

Now, allow's talk about sturdy issue. Think about how you may set your merchandise apart via the usage of unconventional substances. Imagine crafting bracelets from repurposed guitar strings or making jewelry out of vintage buttons. It's all approximately creativity and locating substances that inform a tale.

Quality topics too. A necklace made from tarnish-willing steel or a headband that unravels after one wash might not lessen it. Invest in materials that promise durability, and recollect to remember comfort. If you're designing wearable devices, ensure that your materials are pores and pores and skin-first-class.

Remember, the materials you select need to align together with your logo's identity and values, cater for your target audience's alternatives, and uphold your determination to awesome.

Perfecting Your Product's Design.

Now, permit's talk layout—arguably the coronary coronary heart and soul of your products. Think of your designs as the face of your save, the primary trouble customers be aware. They need to not simplest be visually attractive however moreover useful and unique.

Start by means of sketching your thoughts on paper. Whether it's a hand-drawn example or a virtual mock-up, getting your thoughts down visually is vital. This not handiest allows you refine your idea but additionally serves as a reference for production.

Consider usability. If you are making domestic decor, bear in mind how your portions will wholesome into exquisite dwelling regions. For earrings, ponder how every piece enhances numerous garments. A well-belief-out layout enhances the person revel in and could boom the likelihood of repeat purchases.

Feedback is your pal. Share your designs with trusted friends or mentors and gather their enter. Sometimes, a sparkling pair of eyes can spot upgrades you'll probably have disregarded.

And allow's now not forget about dispositions. While staying proper in your unique style is critical, maintaining an eye constant fixed on market dispositions can deliver your designs a smooth twist. Blend timeless elements with modern-day touches to create products that are each conventional and stylish.

Ensuring Quality and Durability.

Your customers recollect you to supply exceptional merchandise, and that be given as true with should make or damage your Etsy keep's popularity. So, in terms of high-quality and durability, in no way compromise.

Test, test, test! Before list a product, positioned it through rigorous trying out. If you're selling hand-crafted candles, moderate them as lots as make sure they burn calmly. If it is knitwear, check for loose threads or susceptible seams. Don't allow a subpar product attain your customers.

Materials depend right proper here too. High-satisfactory substances not first-rate look and experience higher but additionally stand the take a look at of time. Invest in them, even though it technique adjusting your pricing barely. In the long term, customers are much more likely to pay a chunk greater for products that remaining.

Craftsmanship is essential. Take satisfaction for your artwork and take note of the finer info. Neat sewing, constant clasps, and perfect finishes make all of the difference. Remember, at the same time as customers acquire a product that exceeds their expectations, they'll be much more likely to go away rave reviews and grow to be loyal supporters.

To sum it up, choosing the right materials, perfecting your product's layout, and making sure brilliant and sturdiness are the foundational pillars of crafting impossible to withstand merchandise on your Etsy hold. These elements set the diploma for a a success venture that no longer fine attracts customers but additionally continues them coming again for added.

Now, it's time to location those concepts into motion and create merchandise in order to make your Etsy preserve stand out within the crowded marketplace. Happy crafting!

Subsection 2: Pricing for Profit.

Welcome to the heart of your Etsy adventure – the paintings of pricing your creations for profits. Pricing can be a complex balancing act, however worry not, for I'm right here to guide you thru the intricacies of figuring out the first-class price tag for your hand-crafted gems.

Calculating Production Costs.

To set your Etsy shop up for success, you ought to begin by manner of information your production costs internal and out. This expertise is the foundation upon which your pricing method will rest.

Beginners' Tip: Start with the useful resource of manner of creating an in depth spreadsheet to music each rate, regardless of how small. This consists of now not without a doubt the apparent fees like uncooked materials and shipping prices however moreover the a exquisite deal much less apparent ones like software application payments for your workspace, packaging substances, and listing charges on Etsy. Overlooking these hidden costs can appreciably eat into your income.

Advanced Insights: Break down your costs consistent with unit and calculate how an entire lot you spend on each product. Consider the price of materials, labor (which encompass some time), and every different overhead fees. Don't forget to factor in the share of materials wasted within the direction of producing, similarly to device and device depreciation. For example, in case you make custom hand-stitched leather-based-primarily based bags, element in the fee of every piece of leather-primarily based absolutely, thread, or even the needles used.

Determining a Competitive Pricing Strategy.

Once you have got a strong draw close for your production costs, it's time to determine how you can charge your products competitively. This is in which a piece of market studies comes into play.

Beginners' Tip: Look at what similar products on your area of interest are selling for on Etsy.

What's the not unusual fee issue? This will provide you with a baseline to paintings from. Remember, pricing too excessive might also need to deter capability customers, while pricing too low may additionally moreover make people query the great of your products.

Advanced Insights: Go beyond Etsy and explore other structures and brick-and-mortar stores. Investigate what your opposition are doing, not sincerely with their expenses however also with their marketing and advertising and advertising, packaging, and customer service. Your goal is not just to match their pricing however to stand out in unique strategies even as justifying your charge elements. For instance, in case you're promoting artisanal candles, do not forget what units your candles aside – perhaps it is the usage of herbal elements, precise scents, or personalized labels.

Incorporating Value-Added Pricing.

Value-delivered pricing is wherein you could absolutely shine and maximize your profits. This approach entails such as more rate for your products and charging a pinnacle fee for it.

Beginners' Tip: Think about how you may provide some aspect more for your customers without appreciably growing your costs. It might be as clean as supplying loose present wrapping or a handwritten thank-you phrase with each buy. These small gestures can circulate a protracted manner in delighting your customers and justifying a slightly higher rate thing.

Advanced Insights: Consider growing confined model or excellent products that cater to a selected vicinity of interest or difficulty be counted quantity. This no longer excellent allows you to charge a top price but furthermore creates a revel in of urgency amongst your customers. For instance, if you're a jewelry maker, you can release a unique collection for Valentine's Day with precise designs and packaging.

Remember, pricing is not static. It's a dynamic procedure that evolves as your commercial organization grows and your brand strengthens. Regularly assessment and modify your pricing technique as you benefit experience and accumulate purchaser comments. Always hold the delicate balance between profitability and client price in mind, and you will be nicely to your way to crafting impossible to withstand products that not exceptional sell nicely however moreover assemble a committed purchaser base.

Stay tuned for the following subsection, wherein we'll dive deep into the world of product pics and a way to make your creations look impossible to withstand to capability purchasers.

Subsection 3: Product Photography Mastery.

Welcome to the arena of product pix, wherein the art work of taking images lovely photographs may want to make or wreck your Etsy maintain's achievement. In this bankruptcy, I'll take you thru the quality details of putting in location a rate range-nice images studio, snapping lovable product pics, and sprucing them to perfection.

Setting up a Budget-Friendly Photography Studio.

Picture this: You do now not need a excessive-surrender studio with all of the bells and whistles to take superb product photographs. In truth, you could create a makeshift studio right in your house without breaking the financial organization. Here's how:

1. Find the Perfect Location: Look for a nicely-lit place in your own home, preferably near a window in which herbal moderate floods in. Avoid harsh direct daylight – a sheer curtain can assist diffuse the mild.

2. DIY Backdrops: You don't need pricey backdrops. A clean, impartial-coloured wall, a

piece of fabric, or perhaps a wood table can feature an first-rate history for your products.

three. Lighting: Natural moderate is your super pal, but you could beautify it with low cost device like white foam boards or reflectors. Position them strategically to bop moderate onto your product from distinctive angles.

4. Tripod Stability: Invest in a robust tripod to your digital digital camera or smartphone to ensure constant photographs. This eliminates the chance of shaky, blurry pics.

five. Consistency is Key: Keep your setup constant for all your product pics. This allows in developing a cohesive and professional look for your Etsy save.

Capturing Eye-Catching Product Images.

Now, allow's dive into the paintings of taking pix those charming product snap shots:

1. Clean and Prep: Before you start taking pix, make certain your products are clean and in

pristine state of affairs. Remove any dirt, fingerprints, or imperfections.

2. Camera Settings: Whether you are the use of a DSLR or a telephone, knowledge your digital digicam settings is critical. Experiment with aperture, ISO, and shutter pace to get the appropriate publicity.

three. Composition: Consider the guideline of thumb of thirds. Position your product barely off-middle to create a visually attractive composition. Experiment with one of a kind angles to expose off your product's first rate capabilities.

4. Focus and Depth of Field: Use the autofocus characteristic in your digital camera to make sure your product is sharply in interest. Play with the intensity of discipline to attain a blurred ancient beyond (bokeh) that makes your product pop.

5. Tripod Use: If you are taking snap shots in low moderate conditions or with a sluggish shutter pace, a tripod is essential to avoid

digital digital digicam shake. It ensures sharp, professional-searching photographs.

Editing Photos for a Professional Look.

Now which you've captured some exquisite product pictures, it is time to enhance them similarly:

1. Choose the Right Software: There are many photograph enhancing device to be had, from unfastened alternatives like GIMP and Canva to paid packages like Adobe Photoshop and Lightroom. Select one that fits your needs and fee variety.

2. Crop and Resize: Crop your pictures to put off distractions and resize them to in form Etsy's photo necessities. A everyday length is 2000x2000 pixels for a square product image.

three. Color Correction: Adjust brightness, evaluation, and saturation to make your product's shades pop. Correct any coloration casts or inconsistencies.

4. Background Removal: Use system much like the magic wand or pen tool to take away the heritage if needed. A smooth, white historical past is frequently preferred for product pics.

five. Save and Optimize: Save your photos inside the right format (JPEG is ideal for net) and optimize them for internet use to ensure speedy loading instances to your Etsy store.

Remember, exercise makes high-quality. Experiment with one-of-a-kind lighting, angles, and improving strategies until you discover the style that fits your brand and merchandise splendid. Consistency on your product images will not quality make your Etsy hold look professional but additionally help construct recollect with potential clients. So, draw close your digital camera, installation your DIY studio, and permit your merchandise shine via the lens. Your Etsy empire is one fascinating photo away!

Subsection four: Crafting Compelling Product Listings.

Crafting compelling product listings is corresponding to casting a spell on capacity customers, drawing them nearer with each word and image. In this phase, we're going to delve deep into the artwork of seduction, as we discover a manner to write down persuasive product titles and descriptions, harness the magic of key phrases for are searching for optimization, and highlight your specific selling elements like a beacon in a crowded marketplace.

Writing Persuasive Product Titles and Descriptions.

Your product identify is your first risk to capture a functionality purchaser's hobby, and the outline is in that you seal the deal. So, allow's reason them to every no longer feasible to withstand.

Tip for Beginners: Start with clarity and ease. Your understand need to definitely bring what your product is, the usage of sincere language. If you are selling home made soy candles, a call like "Hand-Poured Lavender Scented Soy Candle" does the technique.

Advanced Techniques: Once you've got nailed the basics, it's time to sprinkle a few fairy dust. Use electricity words that evoke emotions and interest. Instead of just "Hand-Poured Lavender Scented Soy Candle," try "Elevate Your Senses with Our Handcrafted Lavender Bliss Soy Candle." See the distinction? You've sincerely brought a touch of luxury and pleasure.

Now, allow's dive into descriptions. Paint a photo with phrases. Describe not definitely the product, however the enjoy it offers. How does it experience, fragrance, or taste? What issues does it treatment? Who would love it? For that Lavender Bliss Soy Candle, you can say, "Indulge within the soothing aroma of our Lavender Bliss Soy Candle, hand-poured with love to create a tranquil surroundings in your own home. Escape the chaos of the day because the calming lavender scent wraps you in a cocoon of serenity."

Utilizing Relevant Keywords for Search Optimization.

Keywords are the name of the sport sauce to visibility on Etsy. To maintain close this, you want to anticipate like a customer. Imagine you are searching for a very precise piece of hand-painted pottery. What phrases might you type into Etsy's searching for bar? Those are your key terms.

Tip for Beginners: Start with considerable, stylish key terms that describe your product class. For the hand-painted pottery, use "ceramic vase" or "artisan pottery."

Advanced Techniques: Now, allow's dive into prolonged-tail key phrases. These are unique terms that potential customers might also use. For example, "hand-painted blue and white ceramic vase" or "boho-stimulated pottery decor." Etsy's search algorithm loves those gem stones due to the fact they in shape what humans are looking for.

Do some key-word research the usage of tools like Google's Keyword Planner or Etsy's are attempting to find bar itself. It'll unveil the golden nuggets people are typing in.

Highlighting Unique Selling Points.

In the large sea of Etsy stores, what sets yours apart? This is wherein your specific promoting factors (USPs) shine.

Tip for Beginners: Identify what makes your product special. Is it hand-crafted, inexperienced, customizable, or regionally sourced? Whatever it is, shout it from the digital rooftops. Include it in your product descriptions, and keep in mind to mention it to your keep's "About" segment.

Advanced Techniques: Let's take the ones USPs and increase them. Paint a sparkly photograph of what devices your product apart. If it is home made, share the tale of the arms that created it. If it's far inexperienced, provide an explanation for how it's miles saving the planet, one buy at a time. Make your customers experience like they're a part of something precise and enormous.

For instance, in case you provide domestic made, organic little one clothing, your product description may likely skip like this: "Wrap your little one inside the softest, hand-stitched herbal cotton. Each piece is a tough paintings of affection, unfastened from chemical compounds, due to the fact your infant deserves no longer some thing however the pleasant. With every purchase, you're supporting a sustainable future on your toddler and the planet."

Crafting irresistible product listings is not quite tons terms; it is about storytelling, emotion, and connection. It's about transforming a mere list into an experience, making your shoppers no longer simply clients, but lovers and advocates of your emblem. Master those techniques, and you may locate your Etsy maintain standing out like a gem in a treasure chest, organized to be discovered and loved via the area.

Subsection 5: Managing Inventory and Orders.

It's a exciting dance of creativity and logistics that may make or smash your save's reputation. So, tighten your apron, and allow's dive into the nitty-gritty of creating your store run like a nicely-oiled device.

Implementing Efficient Inventory Tracking.

Imagine this: You're within the place, crafting your first rate-promoting hand made candles, and orders are rolling in. But wait, do you have got enough lavender-scented wax left? Efficient stock monitoring is the name of the game sauce right here. I can't pressure this sufficient; it is a undertaking-changer.

Start via categorizing your products. Create a spreadsheet list every product, its quantity, and reorder thresholds. Update this frequently, specially after a busy weekend or a a fulfillment social media advertising and advertising advertising campaign.

Consider inventory control gear like QuickBooks, or the unfastened alternatives like Google Sheets. They'll assist you keep tabs in your inventory and ship you reminders at the identical time as it is time to restock components.

Handling Orders, Shipping, and Customer Communication.

Orders are the lifeblood of your store, and every purchaser interplay is an possibility to polish. When to procure an order, ship a pleasant thank-you message. It is going an prolonged way in constructing rapport.

Now, onto shipping! Invest in a reliable postal scale to make sure accurate delivery expenses. Etsy offers shipping labels, making the device smoother. Pro tip: Consider providing bundle deal deal monitoring to provide your customers peace of mind.

Remember, conversation is high. If there's a cast off or hassle with an order, notify your client right away. Most customers are expertise if they will be stored inside the loop. Your responsiveness can turn a probable terrible state of affairs right proper right into a awesome one.

Strategies for Handling Seasonal Fluctuations.

Ah, seasons—they bring about exceptional holidays and, if you're organized, multiplied profits. But furthermore they carry demanding situations. Here are some techniques that will help you journey the seasonal wave:

Early Preparation: Analyze beyond seasonal tendencies in your area of interest. Start growing seasonal products well earlier to keep away from final-minute strain.

Adjust Inventory: Stock up on your bestsellers and decrease stock of items that don't perform properly at some stage in a selected season.

Shipping Deadlines: Communicate smooth transport time limits for excursion orders. Consider offering expedited delivery options.

Decor and Packaging: Spruce up your preserve's look to fit the season. It gives a festive touch and may boom profits.

Promotions: Plan seasonal promotions and discounts to draw excursion customers.

Let's say you sell handmade Christmas adorns. As October rolls round, begin crafting your specific designs. Update your store banner with a snug winter subject matter. Offer a restrained-time good deal for early fowl clients. And recollect to without a doubt speak your transport remaining dates so your customers accumulate their adorns in time for the holidays.

In quit, studying the art of dealing with inventory and orders is like carrying out a symphony. Stay prepared, communicate efficaciously, and adapt to the seasons, and you will no longer first-rate live to tell the story however thrive inside the international of Etsy. Your clients will thank you, and your store's recognition will shine just like the

North Star on a easy wintry weather night time time.

Chapter 3: Mastering Etsy Shop Setup

Subsection 1: Creating a Standout Shop.

In the colorful global of Etsy, in which strong point and creativity reign very high-quality, your keep's appearance is your first have an impact on—a virtual shopfront that beckons internet web page visitors to discover your creations. But how do you create a standout hold that now not only captures hobby but keeps clients coming decrease again for more? Let's dive in.

Customizing Your Shop's Appearance.

Picture this: you're on foot down a bustling road, and you spot a shop with an attention grabbing window display. It piques your interest, and you cannot help however step inner. Your Etsy maintain want to have the same impact on capability clients, and customization is your secret weapon.

1. Banner and Logo: Start with a charming banner and brand that represent your brand. They ought to be cohesive and without delay

carry the essence of your products. If you promote handcrafted earrings, your banner may additionally show off your elegant portions in opposition to a backdrop of antique lace. Your brand want to mirror your signature style.

2. Shop Icon: This small however strong icon appears subsequent to your keep call in are looking for consequences and on cell gadgets. Ensure it's miles recognizable and resonates with your brand.

three. Shop Announcement: Craft a welcoming and informative shop assertion that introduces site visitors on your international. Share a brief tale about your keep, announce any promotions, and make sure to replace it frequently.

four. Featured Listings: Use the "Featured Listings" phase to exhibit your terrific-promoting or most representative products. Keep it easy via updating it to mirror the season or your extremely-present day creations.

5. Shop Sections: Organize your merchandise into store sections. For example, in case you sell home made candles, create sections like "Scented Candles," "Decorative Candles," and "Gift Sets." This makes navigation a breeze.

Optimizing Your Shop Policies.

Now that your shop appears inviting, it's time to set a few ground hints. Clear and sincere hold guidelines not great instill bear in mind however moreover guard both you and your clients.

1. Shipping Policies: Be crystal smooth about your shipping techniques, prices, and processing times. If you provide international delivery, point out that too. Customers appreciate understanding what to expect.

2. Returns and Refunds: Outline your pass once more and refund guidelines. Explain whether or no longer or not you take transport of returns and beneath what

conditions. Always adhere to Etsy's guidelines to hold a excellent provider recognition.

3. Payment Options: Specify the charge methods you receive. Etsy Payments and PayPal are well-known choices. Make it smooth for customers to complete their transactions.

four. Privacy Policy: Craft a privateness insurance that complies with Etsy's tips. Explain the way you cope with customer facts, which builds accept as true with and suggests your willpower to statistics protection.

5. Custom Orders: If you provide custom orders, describe the tool and any additional expenses. This can be a powerful selling element.

Setting Up Shop Sections for Easy Navigation.

Imagine stepping into a store with everything haphazardly piled collectively. Frustrating, right? Well, the identical applies in your Etsy save. Organizing your products into sections is like having neat aisles in a supermarket. Here's the manner to do it correctly:

1. Categories: Begin thru grouping your merchandise into broader classes. If you promote domestic made pottery, you'll likely have classes like "Mugs," "Bowls," and "Vases."

2. Subcategories: For massive shops, don't forget including subcategories. Under "Mugs," you may have "Coffee Mugs" and "Tea Mugs."

three. Seasonal or Limited Edition: Create a separate segment for seasonal or constrained-model gadgets. Shoppers love exclusivity.

4. Best Sellers: Highlight your pinnacle-appearing products in a segment in their very very own. It's a top notch manner to expose off your strengths.

5. Sale Items: If you run profits or promotions, accumulate discounted gadgets in one place to lure bargain hunters.

Customizing your shop's appearance, optimizing your pointers, and installing region keep sections thoughtfully are the foundational steps to growing a standout Etsy keep. Remember, your keep is not truely a place to sell merchandise; it's a digital showcase of your artistry and emblem. Make it an experience that customers might not forget about, and you'll be properly for your manner to Etsy fulfillment.

Subsection 2: Crafting an Appealing About Page.

In this virtual age, where faceless transactions have emerge as the norm, there can be something profoundly magical approximately connecting with customers on a non-public degree. Your Etsy save's "About Page" is your canvas for painting a notable picture of your self, your logo, and the story within the again of all of it. It's your possibility to infuse your preserve with character, developing a magnetic force that draws clients in and maintains them coming once more for extra.

Telling Your Personal and Brand Story.

Think of your About Page because the digital doorway into your revolutionary international. It's the vicinity in which you can introduce your self, percent your journey, and unveil the ardour that fuels your craft. Here, you're not only a supplier; you're a storyteller.

Example: Sarah's Handmade Jewelry.

Meet Sarah, a passionate earrings artist whose love for gems started out as a infant. Her About Page tells the tale of the manner, one sunny afternoon, she stumbled upon a glowing amethyst in her grandmother's attic. That 2nd ignited a lifelong fascination with stones, ultimately foremost to the appearance of her Etsy hold, "GemstoneGlow." Customers aren't just buying earrings; they may be making an investment in Sarah's journey, every piece resonating alongside side her private connection to the stones she works with.

Connecting with Customers on a Personal Level.

Your About Page is the bridge that connects your customers in your craft. It's in that you permit them to in at the little quirks and idiosyncrasies that make your creations unique. Don't be shy approximately sharing your way, your inspirations, or maybe your progressive traumatic conditions. Authenticity is magnetic.

Example: James's Woodworking Wonderland.

James, a draw close craftsman, exhibits on his About Page that he assets reclaimed wood from nearby farms and deserted barns. He talks about the knots, the grains, and the memories embedded in each piece of timber. He even shares the satisfaction of his hold assistant, a playful rescue dog named Rusty, who oversees brilliant manipulate. Customers flock to James's store because of the truth they experience a connection, now not surely to the lovely furniture he makes but to the soul of his craft.

Showcasing Your Passion and Expertise.

Your About Page is the place to shine a highlight on your expertise. Whether you are a pro artisan or a novice crafter, that is wherein you can bring your willpower to your craft and your commitment to nice.

Example: Emily's Handcrafted Ceramics.

Emily's About Page is a testament to her lifelong love affair with clay. She stocks the hours she's spent on the potter's wheel, the countless kiln firings, and the evolution of her signature glazes. Emily's story is not pretty lots ceramics; it's miles about a burning passion for turning clay into paintings. Customers, whether or not or now not or not they may be ceramic fanatics or new to the region of pottery, are interested in Emily's keep due to the reality they trust in her understanding and her unwavering love for her craft.

Your About Page isn't always simply an obligatory segment in your Etsy preserve—it's the coronary heart and soul of your brand. It's wherein you remodel informal net page site visitors into dependable clients. So, at the equal time as you're taking a seat all the manner right down to craft your About Page, bear in mind to be yourself, percent your journey, and permit your passion shine. Because inside the worldwide of Etsy, your story is your maximum valuable asset, and it's far ready to be shared with the area.

Subsection three: Perfecting Your Shop search engine optimization - The Key to Etsy Stardom.

Ah, the allure of Etsy! The opportunity to turn your innovative ardour proper into a thriving business. But wait, within the big Etsy market, how do you're making your products stand out? How do you make certain ability shoppers can discover your maintain amidst the bustling virtual aisles?

The solution lies in reading the art work of Etsy seo (Search Engine Optimization).

In this digital age, records Etsy's are searching for algorithm is your rate tag to visibility and achievement. So, be a part of me as we delve into the depths of search engine optimization sorcery, unlocking the secrets and techniques and strategies as a way to boom your Etsy save to stardom.

Understanding Etsy's Search Algorithm.

Picture this: a capability client sits down at their pc, types in some key terms, and hits "looking for." Within moments, Etsy's set of policies begins offevolved its dance, combing through the masses of heaps of listings to deliver an internet net web page full of merchandise that completely in shape the hunt. How do you make sure your products make the reduce?

Well, Etsy's set of rules takes numerous factors below attention, and you could need to be outstanding friends with they all.

Relevance: The set of rules seems at how well your product fits the quest terms. This way your product discover, description, and tags want to include the important thing terms that your capability shoppers are likely to use.

Quality: Etsy wishes to show its clients the great of the super. This includes factors like your preserve's popularity (those sparkling reviews do depend!), your product's extremely good, or maybe your hold's information of finishing orders on time.

Engagement: The set of regulations notices at the equal time as customers interact together with your listings. If plenty of human beings click on on in your product, desired it, or perhaps purchase it after seeing it in seek results, Etsy takes this as a sign that your product is relevant and attractive.

Listing Completeness: Ensuring you have got were given stuffed out all of your product statistics and carried out all available tags and attributes tells Etsy that your listing is complete and complete.

Seller Location: Etsy considers the area of every the vendor and the client. This permits buyers discover products that can be shipped to their region quick and value correctly.

Conducting Keyword Research.

Now which you've were given a draw near of what Etsy's set of rules craves, it is time to do some detective art work—key-word detective artwork.

Imagine you are promoting domestic made ceramic mugs. Your capability clients would possibly possibly search for "specific coffee mugs," "hand made teacups," or possibly "one-of-a-type pottery." But how do which key terms are the golden keys for your keep's success?

Here's in which key-word studies comes into play.

1. Brainstorm Like a Pro: Begin thru jotting down all of the key terms and phrases that are related to your products. Think approximately what terms a customer might

probably use while looking for what you provide.

2. Explore Etsy's Search Bar: Start typing your capacity key phrases into Etsy's searching for bar. You'll be aware that it offers autocomplete tips. These are the vital thing terms consumers are actively the usage of.

3. Use Keyword Tools: There are plenty of key-word studies tools available on line, which encompass Google's Keyword Planner or Etsy's private device. These tools can come up with insights into key-word popularity and competition.

four. Spy on Your Competitors: Take a peek at what key phrases your a success opposition are the usage of. If it's miles running for them, it might be simply proper for you too.

five. Long-Tail Keywords: Don't forget about the strength of lengthy-tail key terms—the ones longer, greater precise terms. They may also have a fantastic deal plenty much less competition and produce in substantially targeted site visitors.

Remember, it isn't always pretty much locating key phrases; it's miles approximately locating the right key terms that in shape your products and feature a decent searching for amount.

Optimizing Product Listings for Search Visibility.

Now that you've were given your treasure trove of key terms, it's time to sprinkle them strategically in the course of your product listings.

1. Title Triumph: Your product name is your search engine optimization MVP. Include your primary key-word and any relevant secondary key terms. Make it descriptive, concise, and not possible to withstand.

2. Detailed Descriptions: Your product description is in which you could paint a colorful photograph of your item. Incorporate

key terms glaringly, explaining what makes your product unique.

three. Tag Team: Use all available tags and attributes to maximize your list's visibility. Think about synonyms and alternate phrasings to cover all of your bases.

four. Visual Appeal: High-great snap shots are a need to, but don't forget to include your key phrases in picture report names, alt text, and captions. Etsy's set of guidelines seems at the ones too.

five. Pricing Precision: If applicable, include your keywords on your pricing options. For instance, if you sell custom rings, you can offer "Handcrafted Ruby Necklace – $50."

And there you've got it—your Etsy keep is now search engine optimization-optimized and organized to shine in are searching for outcomes. Remember, studying seo is an ongoing technique. Regularly revisit and replace your key terms, display screen your overall performance, and adapt as desired.

Now, bypass forth and conquer Etsy's digital aisles with the magic of search engine optimization! Your save is one step inside the direction of turning into an Etsy sensation.

Subsection 4: Utilizing Etsy Advertising.

Welcome to the arena of Etsy advertising and marketing and advertising, in which you could supercharge your store's visibility and income functionality. In this monetary damage, we're going to delve deep into the art work of making compelling Etsy Ads campaigns, studying the budgeting approach, and uncovering the secrets and techniques and strategies to reading advert overall performance for optimum returns. So, permit's placed on our advertising hats and start crafting the ones no longer possible to stand up to advertisements!

Creating Effective Etsy Ads Campaigns:

Creating classified ads on Etsy may be a exercising-changer to your keep's publicity. To start, pick out your goal listings as it have to be. These need to be your incredible-acting products, individuals who make your coronary heart race with pride. Remember, the crucial factor to a a success marketing marketing campaign is relevance. Your advertisements must align seamlessly with what customers are searching out.

Tips for Beginners:

Begin with a modest ad advertising and marketing advertising marketing campaign rate range to test the waters.

Utilize Etsy's automated targeting function for ease and convenience.

Craft charming ad titles and descriptions that highlight your product's particular selling points.

Expert Insights: Consider the use of guide centered directly to refine your target audience further. For instance, if you promote hand-crafted earrings, you can reason specific key phrases associated with rings patterns, substances, or activities. This precision can result in better conversion fees.

Budgeting and Monitoring Ad Spend:

Budgeting is the coronary coronary coronary heart of your Etsy Ads advertising and marketing and advertising marketing campaign. Start with the aid of setting a each day or weekly rate range which you're cushty with. Etsy permits you to adjust your charge range at any time, so do no longer feel pressured to decide to a fixed amount.

Tips for Beginners:

Start with a conservative finances and frequently growth it as you be conscious wonderful outcomes.

Monitor your each day spend to ensure it aligns along side your finances goals.

Keep an eye constant to your return on advert spend (ROAS) to gauge the effectiveness of your investment.

Expert Insights: Seasoned sellers often allocate a percentage in their trendy profits for advertising. This approach ensures that advertising spend scales surely on the facet of your earnings growth. For example, dedicating 5-10% of your month-to-month earnings to classified ads is a common exercise.

Analyzing Ad Performance and Making Adjustments:

Here's wherein the magic occurs - analyzing and refining your advert campaigns for maximum green consequences.

Tips for Beginners:

Check your Etsy Ads dashboard frequently to display screen clicks, impressions, and conversions.

Experiment with special advert durations and budgets to discover what works excellent for you.

Don't be discouraged via manner of manner of preliminary setbacks; it takes time to refine your technique.

Expert Insights: Dive deeper into your ad analytics. Pay hobby to which key terms and merchandise carry out the top notch. You can alter bids and allocate extra budget to pinnacle-appearing objects on the identical time as optimizing or pausing campaigns that do not yield the popular outcomes.

Use Case - Sarah's Jewelry Boutique:

Sarah, an Etsy supplier, decided to offer Etsy Ads a attempt for her handcrafted gemstone rings. She commenced with a each day rate range of $10 and determined on automatic focused on to attain a broader purpose marketplace. After a month of strolling her advertising campaign, she found that her "Amethyst Earrings" had been getting the maximum clicks and conversions.

With this insight, Sarah decided to allocate greater of her price range to the "Amethyst

Earrings" list and experimented with guide centered on, specially centered on key terms associated with amethyst jewelry. Her ROAS increased substantially, and her Etsy keep began to flourish.

In this subsection, we've got uncovered the secrets and techniques and techniques and techniques to developing effective Etsy Ads campaigns, managing your rate range, and reading universal overall performance. Remember, advertising and marketing on Etsy is an ongoing technique of refinement. By paying near hobby to the records and continuously making adjustments, you will be nicely to your way to Etsy marketing and advertising fulfillment. So, flow ahead and permit your keep shine in the spotlight!

Subsection five: Building Trust with Reviews and Social Proof.

Hey there, fellow Etsy entrepreneur! Welcome to the bankruptcy it really is all about building take delivery of as genuine with together along with your customers via reviews and social evidence. In the large Etsy market, credibility is your thriller weapon, and on this phase, we're going to dive deep right right into a way to wield it efficaciously.

Encouraging Reviews from Satisfied Customers.

Imagine you have got without a doubt made a sale. Your coronary coronary heart skips a beat, and a feel of feat washes over you. But wait, do not allow the moment pass! This is the first-class time to encourage your satisfied customers to head away glowing opinions. Here's how:

Prompt Communication: From the instantaneous an order is placed, make certain your customer service recreation is on component. Respond to inquiries immediately, offer transport updates, and be attentive. Happy customers are more likely to move away effective comments.

Quality Products: The basis of right reviews is a stellar product. Deliver what you promise, or even exceed expectations if feasible. When your clients are pleased with what they acquire, they'll be willing to sing your praises.

Polite Request: Don't hesitate to kindly ask for a observe. Include a customized word with every order, expressing your gratitude for his or her assist and with courtesy inviting them to percentage their thoughts.

Handling Negative Reviews Professionally.

Now, permit's address the elephant in the Etsy room - terrible reviews. They show as much as the exquisite oldsters, however it's miles the way you deal with them that virtually matters. Here's your damage manage approach:

Stay Calm and Collected: When you acquire a lousy assessment, take a deep breath. Avoid responding emotionally. Instead, respond professionally and with courtesy. Offer a solution or a evidence, usually with the cause to treatment the problem.

Learn and Improve: Negative evaluations may be golden nuggets of belief. Use them as constructive remarks to beautify your merchandise or customer service. Show capability customers which you're devoted to boom.

Follow Etsy's Policies: Familiarize yourself with Etsy's tips on comments. In some instances, if a assessment violates the ones suggestions, you may request its removal.

Leveraging Social Media for Customer Testimonials.

In current digital age, social media is your megaphone for spreading the word about your Etsy hold. Here's how you can leverage it to accumulate and show off purchaser testimonials:

Create Shareable Content: Craft attractive posts supplying your products and happy customers. Encourage your customers to percentage their non-public images and memories related to your objects.

Use Hashtags: Use applicable hashtags to boom the discoverability of your posts. For example, in case you sell hand-crafted candles, use hashtags like #HandmadeCandles or #EtsyFinds.

Engage and Repost: Interact on the side of your clients on social media. Respond to feedback, thank them for their assist, and preserve in thoughts to invite for permission to repost their content cloth cloth. User-generated content fabric is a effective recall builder.

Run Giveaways and Contests: Host giveaways or contests that require people to percent their tales together collectively with your merchandise. This now not best generates buzz however additionally gives you with smooth testimonials.

Create Instagram Stories Highlights: Use Instagram's Stories Highlights characteristic to curate consumer testimonials. It's an effects accessible show off for functionality shoppers.

In conclusion, critiques and social evidence are your high-quality buddies within the international of Etsy. They set up receive as actual with, show off your merchandise, and join you with a community of reliable clients. Remember, constructing maintain in thoughts takes time, so be affected character and persistent. Encourage critiques, manage terrible remarks gracefully, and harness the energy of social media to growth your Etsy achievement story. Your thriving shop is only a few well-placed critiques and social media shares away!

Chapter 4: Marketing Your Etsy Shop

Subsection 1: Harnessing the Power of Social Media.

When it consists of advertising your Etsy keep, one of the most powerful gadget on your arsenal is social media. Social systems offer an awesome possibility to connect to your target marketplace, show off your products, and construct a devoted following. In this phase, I'm going to stroll you via the method of creating a prevailing social media advertising and marketing plan, choosing the proper structures for your region of hobby, and gaining knowledge of the artwork of crafting engaging content material cloth and visuals.

Creating a Social Media Marketing Plan.

Imagine your social media advertising and advertising plan due to the fact the blueprint on your Etsy save's on-line presence. It's not about posting aimlessly; it is approximately having a smooth method in vicinity. Here's the way to create a plan that works:

1. Set Clear Goals: Start through defining your desires. Are you trying to increase emblem consciousness, power site visitors in your Etsy shop, or boom income? Knowing your goals will manual your efforts.

2. Know Your Audience: Understanding your target market is prime. Who are your pleasant clients? What are their interests, pain factors, and behaviors? Tailor your content material to resonate with them.

three. Choose the Right Platforms: Not all social media structures are created equal. Pinterest may work wonders for home made earrings, whilst Instagram might be nice for showcasing your art prints. Research wherein your target audience hangs out.

4. Content Calendar: Plan your posts in advance. A content material calendar ensures which you always supply valuable content cloth fabric. It's like having a roadmap for your social media adventure.

5. Engagement Strategy: Don't simply post and disappear. Engage collectively together along with your target marketplace via the usage of responding to comments, asking questions, and provoking discussions. Build relationships, not sincerely fanatics.

Choosing the Right Platforms for Your Niche.

Different structures cater to specific audiences and product types. Here's a short rundown:

1. Instagram: Ideal for visual merchandise. Use incredible pics and memories to reveal off your creations. Explore the arena of hashtags to expand your reap.

2. Pinterest: Perfect for DIY and craft merchandise. Create desirable pins and forums associated with your area of hobby. Pinterest is a goldmine for sharing tutorials and concept.

3. Facebook: A flexible platform for all sorts of merchandise. Utilize Facebook

organizations, create a enterprise net web page, and do not forget jogging targeted commercials to attain ability customers.

4. Twitter: Great for sharing updates and attractive in conversations. Use relevant hashtags and participate in trending topics to benefit visibility.

five. TikTok: Rising in popularity for showcasing hand-crafted merchandise. Short, exciting movement pics can short clutch interest and energy site visitors to your store.

Crafting Engaging Content and Visuals.

Now, permit's communicate approximately the coronary coronary heart of your social media technique: content material material cloth and visuals.

1. Tell a Story: Share the story inside the back of your merchandise. People want to realize the foundation, method, and passion in the decrease lower back of what they'll be shopping for.

2. Visual Consistency: Maintain a constant seen fashion in your posts. Use filters, shades, and fonts that align together at the side of your emblem.

three. Video Content: Videos are king on social media. Create product demos, inside the lower lower back of-the-scenes glimpses, and tutorials to interact your target marketplace.

4. User-Generated Content: Encourage your customers to percent their critiques together together with your products. Repost their content material with right credit score score score—it's miles right and builds remember.

5. CTA (Call to Action): Always encompass a clean call to motion to your posts. Whether it's "Shop Now," "Learn More," or "Tag a Friend," manual your target audience on what to do subsequent.

Case Study: Jenny's Handmade Ceramics.

Meet Jenny, an Etsy dealer who creates amazing home made ceramics. She decided to recognition her social media efforts on Instagram and Pinterest. Jenny's method end up to put up a mixture of product pics, technique films, and manner of lifestyles images that featured her ceramics in real-lifestyles settings, along with cushty breakfast nooks and stylish dinner tables.

She engaged together together with her lovers via taking walks giveaways and asking questions like, "What's your selected ceramic color?" She furthermore collaborated with micro-influencers who shared her love for artisanal domestic decor.

Over time, Jenny's social media following grew gradually, and her Etsy save skilled a giant enhance in visitors and earnings. Her regular branding and engaging content material material cloth grew to emerge as her social media presence right into a magnet for ceramic fanatics.

Remember, your social media adventure may additionally additionally require staying electricity, but with the proper technique, you can turn your Etsy keep right right into a recognizable emblem with a committed following. So, start crafting that plan, select out your structures correctly, and permit your creativity shine thru appealing content material cloth and visuals. The international of social media is your oyster, and your Etsy maintain is the pearl equipped to be found.

Subsection 2: Email Marketing for Etsy.

Ah, e mail marketing – the unsung hero of a hit Etsy shops. If you are prepared to loose up the whole capability of your Etsy organization, you are in for a cope with. In this chapter, we are able to delve deep into the arena of e-mail advertising and advertising and marketing and advertising, a effective tool that can help you construct patron relationships, pressure earnings, and preserve your hold inside the highlight. Join me in this adventure as we find out 3 important elements of e-mail advertising and marketing: building and segmenting your electronic mail listing, crafting compelling e-mail campaigns, and measuring electronic mail advertising success.

Building and Segmenting Your Email List.

Imagine having a set of devoted customers who eagerly expect your emails, geared up to grab up your contemporary-day day merchandise. That's the magic of a properly-crafted electronic mail listing. But first, you want subscribers.

Tips for Beginners:

Start with what you have got. Gather emails from pals, family, and current-day clients.

Create an now not possible to resist lead magnet. Offer a reduction, loose guide, or wonderful get right of get right of entry to to to draw capability subscribers.

Utilize Etsy's covered electronic mail advertising and marketing device to collect patron emails and section your list automatically.

Expert Insights: Once you have amassed a considerable list, it is time to section. Divide your subscribers based totally totally on their opportunities, buy history, or place. Why? Segmented emails electricity fifty 8% of all sales. For example, in case you sell home made earrings, phase your listing to deliver customized emails to clients who have previously sold necklaces while you release a trendy necklace collection.

Crafting Compelling Email Campaigns.

Now which you've were given your subscribers coated up, it's time to create content material material material that speaks right away to their hearts and wallets. Crafting an not possible to face up to electronic mail marketing campaign is an artwork shape.

Tips for Beginners:

Start clean. Craft a welcome electronic mail series that introduces new subscribers to your keep, shares your story, and gives a unique good buy.

Be regular. Create a content material fabric material calendar so your subscribers recognize even as to assume your emails.

Keep it seen. Use superb photographs of your products and make your emails visually attractive.

Expert Insights: Let's speak approximately storytelling. Imagine you sell hand-painted domestic decor. Instead of sending an everyday email approximately your ultra-contemporary arrivals, inform a story approximately the way you decided your passion for portray, the approach on the decrease again of each piece, and the feelings you reason to awaken. Weave your merchandise into the narrative, making them a part of an emotional journey.

Measuring Email Marketing Success.

How do you recognize if your email marketing and advertising efforts are paying off? The solution lies in data. By reading key metrics, you can refine your strategies for optimum effect.

Tips for Beginners:

Start with fundamental metrics like open expenses, click on on-thru expenses, and unsubscribe fees. These will let you recognise how appealing your emails are.

Pay interest to conversion prices – the share of subscribers who make a purchase after clicking in your e mail.

Track sales generated from electronic mail campaigns. This is the very last degree of success.

Expert Insights: Get granular collectively collectively along with your evaluation. Dive into email heatmaps to peer in which subscribers are clicking. A heatmap ought to in all likelihood show that maximum clicks rise up on product pics. Capitalize on this perception thru which includes extra product snap shots for your emails.

Remember, e mail advertising and marketing and advertising and marketing and advertising and marketing is a adventure, not a vacation spot. Continuously take a look at and tweak your strategies based totally mostly on the facts you got. Experiment with challenge strains, e mail timing, and content material to look what resonates splendid along with your target marketplace.

In surrender, email marketing is your secret weapon to expand your Etsy save beyond your wildest dreams. Whether you are sincerely starting or trying to level up, constructing and segmenting your electronic mail list, crafting compelling electronic mail campaigns, and measuring fulfillment will set you at the path to Etsy stardom. So, start crafting those emails and watch your Etsy empire flourish!

Subsection 3: Collaborations and Partnerships.

Picture this: You're the captain of a deliver, sailing the massive virtual seas of Etsy. But to absolutely thrive, you cannot move it on my own; you want allies, co-captains, and fellow adventurers. In this bankruptcy, we are diving deep into the art of collaborations and partnerships. We'll find out how you can accomplice with influencers, group up with other Etsy sellers, and create collaborations that advantage all and sundry worried.

Partnering with Influencers: Unleash the Power of Influence.

In the age of social media, influencers are the cutting-edge-day trendsetters, the Pied Pipers of our virtual global. They have the potential to sway opinions, create tendencies, and, most importantly, strength potential customers for your Etsy store.

Imagine you sell hand made jewelry, and you're collaborating with a style influencer stated for his or her exquisite taste. They function your jewelry of their Instagram reminiscences, sporting it with style and flair.

Suddenly, your Etsy store tales a surge in visitors, and orders start pouring in.

Here's how you could make influencer partnerships come up with the results you need:

1. Identify the Right Influencers: Look for influencers whose audience aligns collectively along with your purpose marketplace. Tools like Instagram and TikTok analytics will allow you to discover influencers with demographics that during form your exceptional clients.

2. Build Genuine Relationships: Approach influencers with sincerity. Send a personal message expressing your admiration for his or her art work and why you receive as genuine together along with your merchandise can also resonate with their target audience.

3. Offer Value: Be organized to offer influencers with unfastened samples of your merchandise or compensation for his or her

effort and time. Remember, this is an funding on your industrial business enterprise.

four. Set Clear Expectations: Outline the terms of your collaboration, which include the kind of content material material material, posting agenda, and any hashtags or links you need them to embody.

Joint Promotions and Cross-Selling: Strength in Numbers.

Collaborating with other Etsy sellers can be a sport-changer for your store. Think of it as a together beneficial partnership, in that you be a part of forces to gain a much wider purpose marketplace.

Suppose you create home made scented candles, and each extraordinary Etsy supplier makes a speciality of fantastically crafted candle holders. Together, you may create themed gift devices, imparting a reduction whilst customers buy each your merchandise. This skip-promoting approach now not first-rate will boom your sales but furthermore enhances the purchasing for experience in your customers.

Here's the way to make joint promotions and skip-selling paintings:

1. Find Complementary Sellers: Seek out Etsy dealers whose merchandise supplement yours. You do not want direct competitors; as an possibility, aim for synergy.

2. Plan Themed Collaborations: Brainstorm innovative mind for joint promotions. Consider vacations, seasons, or trends that align collectively along side your products.

three. Create Exclusive Bundles: Craft unique bundles or programs that combine your products. Offer those at a very particular charge to entice customers.

4. Promote Together: Collaborate on advertising and advertising and advertising and marketing efforts. Share each super's merchandise on social media, newsletters, or maybe for your Etsy save bulletins.

Creating Win-Win Collaborations: The Secret Sauce.

The key to successful collaborations is ensuring that everybody concerned advantages. A win-win collaboration not great boosts profits but additionally fosters outstanding relationships in the Etsy community.

For instance, let's say you're a antique clothing dealer, and also you associate with a close-by artist who designs custom garb patches. You determine to host a joint event at a community craft sincere, wherein customers can buy your vintage clothes and customise them with the artist's patches immediate. This collaboration no longer super generates income however also creates a memorable revel in for clients.

Here's the way to create win-win collaborations:

1. Understand Shared Goals: Discuss along with your collaborators what you each

choice to acquire from the partnership. Align your desires.

2. Leverage Each Other's Networks: Tap into each different's customer bases and social media followings to maximise publicity.

3. Communicate Effectively: Keep the strains of communication open and obvious. Regularly test in in conjunction with your collaborators to make sure definitely all people is on the equal page.

4. Celebrate Successes: When your collaboration yields powerful consequences, have an amazing time them together. Share your achievements together with your target audience to expose off the charge of your partnership.

Collaborations and partnerships are like wind inside the sails of your Etsy keep. They can propel your enterprise to new heights, join you with new customers, and infuse smooth energy into your emblem. So, acquire out, construct relationships, and set sail on this interesting journey of modern cooperation. Your Etsy empire will thanks for it.

Subsection four: Etsy Promotions and Sales.

Welcome to the advertising and marketing and marketing and advertising and marketing playground of Etsy! In this dynamic subsection, we're diving deep into Etsy Promotions and Sales Events. Think of it as your mystery weapon for enhancing profits, gaining visibility, and developing a buzz round your hold.

Running Successful Sales and Discounts.

Picture this: You stroll into your favourite hold, and a neon sign screams "50% OFF TODAY!" How not possible to face as much as does that sound? Well, you can create that identical exhilaration on your Etsy hold.

Tip #1: Timing is Everything - Consider strolling profits for the duration of holidays, precise activities, or maybe to your save's anniversary. It's a surefire way to draw hobby. For instance, a "Back to School Sale" in August or a "Spring Clearance" in April can art work wonders.

Tip #2: Bundle Deals and BOGO Offers - Everyone loves a good buy. Offering "Buy One, Get One 50% Off" or growing product bundles with a reduction can beautify your average order fee.

Tip #three: Flash Sales - These are the coronary heart-pounding, limited-time gives that maintain customers coming decrease again. Try walking a 24-hour flash sale or a weekend good buy to create a sense of urgency.

Tip #4: Abandoned Cart Discounts - Ever had a client nearly entire their buy however then abandon their cart? Send them a moderate nudge with a discount code to encourage them to finish the transaction.

Participating in Etsy-Specific Promotions.

Etsy offers severa promotional equipment to help you shine in their market. One of these is

Etsy Ads, a pay-consistent with-click on on on marketing provider.

Tip #five: Etsy Ads - With Etsy Ads, you may showcase your products on the pinnacle of are seeking results. Set a price range, pick out out out your goal key phrases, and watch your shop bounce. Monitor the general overall performance and adjust your finances as favored.

Tip #6: Etsy Offsite Ads - Etsy additionally gives Offsite Ads, that could make bigger your attain beyond Etsy itself. When your product is featured on Google, Bing, and different systems, you pay a referral rate best at the same time as you are making a sale from the ones classified ads.

Strategies for Holiday and Seasonal Sales.

Holidays and changing seasons are excessive time for Etsy dealers. Shoppers are looking for unique presents and seasonal decor. Here's the way to make the maximum of those opportunities:

Tip #7: Themed Collections - Curate a group of products specially tailored to the vacation or season. For example, if it is Valentine's Day, create a "Love and Romance" series together together with your maximum romantic objects.

Tip #8: Decorate Your Shop - Change your keep banner, profile photo, and product images to reflect the vacation or season. It provides a festive touch and suggests you are within the spirit.

Tip #9: Countdown Promotions - Build anticipation with the beneficial useful resource of counting all of the manner down to the holiday with every day or weekly promotions. Offer a extraordinary deal or product each day to keep customers engaged.

Tip #10: Offer Gift Wrapping - Make excursion searching for simpler for your customers with the aid of using offering gift wrapping as an opportunity. Many customers are inclined to pay a touch more for the benefit.

Now, do not forget, advertising and advertising and advertising is an art work as masses as it's far a generation. What works for one preserve may not art work for a few other, so don't be afraid to test, song your outcomes, and refine your strategies. Etsy is a colourful, ever-converting market, and with the right advertising method, your hold can thrive and stand happy with the group.

So flow beforehand, plan those earnings, encompass Etsy promotions, and make each tour season your terrific one but. Your Etsy empire is at the upward push!

Subsection five: Analyzing Your Marketing Efforts.

As you embark for your adventure to Etsy stardom, there can be one critical difficulty of the technique that can not be omitted: reading your advertising and advertising and marketing efforts. It's like navigating a deliver thru uncharted waters; you want to test your path frequently to ensure you are on the right music. In this subsection, we're going to delve deep into the artwork of interpreting advertising and marketing metrics, tweaking your technique for higher outcomes, or perhaps dive into some real-life case research of a success Etsy keep advertising and advertising campaigns that became the tides in need in their captains.

Tracking and Analyzing Marketing Metrics.

Imagine this: you have got set sail, but you're blindfolded. How will you realise in case you're shifting inside the right course? The identical is going for your Etsy preserve advertising and advertising and marketing and advertising efforts. To navigate your way to achievement, you need statistics. Here's how you could gather and interpret it:

Conversion Rate: This is the proportion of site visitors who make a buy on your keep. Track it to look how powerful your product listings and outlines are. If your conversion fee is low, maintain in thoughts enhancing your product presentation or focused on a amazing goal marketplace.

Click-Through Rate (CTR): CTR tells you what number of people clicked in your product listings after seeing them. A excessive CTR shows that your titles and pics are compelling. If it's far low, you can want to optimize your listings for higher visibility.

Return on Investment (ROI): Calculate how plenty cash you've got crafted from your advertising and marketing efforts in evaluation to what you spent. This enables you pick out which advertising and marketing channels are maximum profitable and in which to allocate your finances.

Traffic Sources: Understand wherein your internet web page traffic are coming from - whether or now not it's far organic are trying to find, social media, or advertisements. This allow you to hobby on the pleasant advertising and advertising channels.

Customer Acquisition Cost (CAC): Determine how a whole lot it charges to acquire a cutting-edge consumer. If your CAC is truly too excessive, you would probably need to refine your focused on or advertising and advertising technique.

Adjusting Your Marketing Strategy for Better Results.

Once you have got this treasure trove of data, it is time to chart a present day course or excellent-song your modern one. Here are a few strategies to preserve in mind:

A/B Testing: Experiment with one in each of a type product pics, titles, or advert reproduction to appearance what resonates notable together with your audience. Small adjustments can yield massive consequences.

Budget Optimization: Based in your ROI, allocate your advertising price range to the maximum worthwhile channels. Don't be afraid to reduce on underperforming ones.

Seasonal Adjustments: Etsy purchasing for developments can variety through season. Analyze beyond facts to anticipate and capitalize on those trends with properly timed promotions and listings.

Target Audience Refinement: If your metrics display that your cutting-edge purpose marketplace isn't changing well, revisit your patron personas. Adjust your advertising and marketing and advertising and advertising to target a greater receptive purpose market.

Case Studies of Successful Etsy Shop Marketing Campaigns.

Let's sail into some real-worldwide success recollections to illustrate those thoughts:

Case Study 1: "HandmadeHeirlooms"

HandmadeHeirlooms, an Etsy save focusing on custom-made vintage-inspired earrings, preferred to beautify its vacation sales. They analyzed their beyond records and determined that Pinterest end up riding a big quantity of web site visitors however had a lower conversion charge compared to big channels.

Their answer? They ran a Pinterest-particular marketing and advertising, providing a limited-time reduce fee to Pinterest clients.

This introduced about a splendid increase in conversions from Pinterest site visitors at a few level within the excursion season.

Case Study 2: "CraftyPrints"

CraftyPrints, a store selling customizable artwork prints, found that their CTR on Google Ads had dropped considerably. After A/B finding out first rate ad headlines and pictures, they determined that easier, more visually attractive commercials finished better. By making these changes, they not high-quality improved CTR but additionally noticed an growth in wellknown profits.

These case studies showcase the energy of records-driven choice-making and the capacity for boom even as you're inclined to conform your method primarily based totally on the insights you obtain.

In give up, as a savvy Etsy entrepreneur, in no way underestimate the significance of studying your advertising and advertising metrics and making data-knowledgeable alternatives. It's the compass which could steer your shop closer to the seashores of achievement. So, hoist your sails, gather your records, and chart your path to Etsy greatness. Fair winds and satisfied selling!

Chapter 5: Delivering Exceptional Customer Service

Subsection 1: Setting Customer Expectations.

As I delved deeper into the area of going for walks a a achievement Etsy preserve, I speedy positioned out that one of the cornerstones of constructing a sturdy and sustainable business corporation became handing over super customer support. It's no longer quite an entire lot selling merchandise; it's far about developing an unforgettable buying experience that maintains clients coming lower lower again for added. In this financial ruin, we're going to cognizance on the first step in achieving that motive: setting client expectancies.

Creating Clear Shop Policies.

Imagine taking walks right right into a physical keep and now not expertise whether or now not you can cross back a product, what price techniques are big, or how lengthy it'll take in your purchase to reach. That could be tense, right? The equal precept applies in your Etsy hold. Your clients need to realize what to expect after they keep with you.

Start with the aid of crafting clean and concise preserve pointers. These must cover everything from shipping and returns to fee strategies and your keep's assignment. Think of those suggestions as the inspiration of your customer support approach. They set the regulations of engagement amongst you and your customers.

For example, if you sell home made jewelry, your guidelines would possibly probable encompass info at the substances used, sizing statistics, and your commitment to green packaging. By offering this facts in advance, you are no longer great ensuring transparency but also building accept as true with collectively collectively along with your clients.

Managing Customer Inquiries and Messages.

Communication is pinnacle in any dating, and your dating together with your clients isn't always any exception. When clients have questions or concerns, they expect set off and useful responses. Failure to acquire this will result in out of region profits and damaged recognition.

To live on pinnacle of purchaser inquiries and messages, set aside committed time each day to test your Etsy messages. Responding in a well timed way is critical, regardless of the truth that the message is a easy "thanks" for a modern buy. It shows that you care about your customers and their revel in.

Now, allow's talk approximately dealing with inquiries and worries. Consider this situation: a client contacts you because of the truth they acquired a broken item. First, precise empathy and make an apology for the inconvenience. Then, offer a solution— whether or not or now not or now not it is a opportunity, refund, or pass lower back commands. Remember, customer service is not quite lots problem-solving; it is approximately turning terrible evaluations into powerful ones.

Communicating Shipping Times and Tracking Information.

Shipping can be a make-or-wreck 2nd in the client journey. Your clients want to understand when they will gather their purchases, and they'll be eager for updates along the way. This is wherein clear communique turns into vital.

Start by way of using putting realistic shipping expectations. If you provide domestic made objects, consider the time it takes to create them, and component that into your predicted delivery instances. It's higher to underpromise and overdeliver than the other way around.

When a patron makes a purchase, proper away deliver them a shipping confirmation with monitoring facts. This no longer amazing maintains them inside the loop however additionally offers a experience of safety.

They can display their package deal's adventure and recognize precisely even as it will arrive.

For example, if you promote custom paintings, you would probably say, "Your unique painting can be organized to supply in 2-3 weeks, and you will acquire monitoring statistics as quick because it's on its way."

In my very non-public Etsy journey, I've visible how setting smooth expectancies, coping with messages with care, and speaking transport information transformed occasional purchasers into reliable customers. It's not pretty much the product you promote; it's far approximately the experience you offer. When customers apprehend they'll take delivery of as right with you, they may be much more likely to move back for added purchases and suggest your save to others. So, preserve in thoughts, the muse of extremely good customer service starts offevolved with placing the proper expectations.

Subsection 2: Handling Customers.

Ah, purchaser remarks – the lifeblood of any a success Etsy shop. It's like navigating a rollercoaster: exhilarating highs whilst you got glowing reward and nerve-wracking plunges whilst confronted with criticism. In this phase, I'm going to expose you the way to journey this rollercoaster with grace and flip even the maximum horrible comments right into a golden possibility.

Managing Both Positive and Negative Feedback.

Let's begin with the great things: extremely good remarks. It's a testomony in your hard artwork and self-discipline. When you get preserve of a rave assessment, don't surely permit it sit down down there like a trophy on a shelf. Engage with it! Respond with actual gratitude. A smooth "Thank you loads in your kind phrases! We're thrilled you want our product!" is going a protracted way. You're now not in reality acknowledging the purchaser; you're developing a tremendous connection that would bring about repeat business.

Now, brace your self for the not-so-tremendous comments. Negative reviews can sting, but remember, they are opportunities in cowl. First and principal, do no longer take it for my part. Take a deep breath and take a look at the criticism objectively. Is there a real problem along facet your products or services that goals addressing? If so, widely recognized it. Respond professionally and empathetically. Say some difficulty like, "I'm sorry to pay interest approximately your experience. We take your feedback severely and will do the whole thing to make it proper."

Turning Negative Experiences into Opportunities.

Turning lemons into lemonade isn't only a cliché; it's miles a customer service method. Use terrible feedback as a catalyst for development. Imagine this: A purchaser complains about the stitching on a handmade bag coming unfastened. Instead of seeing it as a failure, view it as an possibility to beautify your product. Respond, "I make an apology for the inconvenience. We've taken steps to improve our sewing manner, and I'd like to deliver you a substitute bag to make up for the trouble." You no longer simplest salvage a customer relationship however furthermore show off your dedication to fantastic.

Sometimes, the hassle isn't always together together with your product however a misconception. Clear the air with endurance and allure. A customer could probable say, "This isn't the colour I expected!" Instead of having protective, respond, "I'm sorry for any confusion. Colors can range on video display units, but we're going to do our best to fit your expectations next time. Let's communicate how we're able to make this right for you presently."

Responding Professionally and Empathetically.

Your response to feedback want to usually be expert and empathetic. Even if a customer's criticism feels unjust, keep away from arguing or being shielding. Your Etsy keep's recognition is on the street. Maintain your cool and cope with the trouble constructively.

For example, if a client claims that their order did not arrive on time, don't say, "It's not our fault; blame the postal provider!" Instead, say, "I'm sorry for the transport postpone you professional. Let's art work together to discover a answer, whether or no longer it definitely is monitoring the bundle deal or sending a opportunity."

Remember, capability clients observe these interactions. By coping with them gracefully, you are showcasing your dedication to top notch customer service. It's a reflection of your emblem's character.

In end, feedback is a present, and every piece — nice or poor — is a threat to develop and enhance your Etsy store. Embrace it, reply professionally, and turn the ones hard moments into possibilities for greatness. Your customers will recognize your dedication, and your Etsy keep will thrive because of it.

Subsection three: Shipping and Packaging Best Practices.

Ah, the immediately your customer hits that "Buy Now" button, your coronary heart skips a beat. You've crafted the proper product, dazzled them together together together with your Etsy keep, and now it is time to deliver that exceptional bundle deal into their keen arms. But how will you make certain that the transport and packaging technique lives as a lot because the rest of your customer experience? That's what we're approximately to delve into.

Efficient Shipping Methods and Carriers.

Shipping is the bridge amongst your online introduction and your patron's real-worldwide delight. Choosing the proper transport method and issuer must make or wreck your client's revel in. Here's a manner to do it proper:

Tip 1: Know Your Options.

Before you may pick out the excellent method and provider, you want to understand your alternatives. The most common techniques encompass preferred delivery, expedited shipping, and global shipping. Carriers like USPS, FedEx, UPS, and DHL offer severa offerings. Understand their prices, transport instances, and monitoring abilties.

Tip 2: Consider Your Product.

The nature of your product topics. If you're promoting touchy hand-blown glass embellishes, you may need a provider with a reputation for moderate handling. If you're selling virtual prints, precedence might be rapid delivery.

Tip 3: Offer Options to Customers.

Give your customers selections. Offer a few delivery options at simply one in all a type rate elements and be obvious about predicted delivery times. Customers love alternatives, and it can help you cater to specific budgets.

Eco-Friendly Packaging Options.

Now that you've looked after out your shipping logistics, allow's communicate about packaging. Not first-rate does it defend your precious creations, but it's also a danger to show your dedication to the surroundings.

Tip 1: Recycled Materials.

Choose packaging materials crafted from recycled materials. There are eco-friendly alternatives for the entirety from bubble wrap to packing peanuts. Show your customers you care approximately the planet.

Tip 2: Minimalist Design

Go minimalist together along with your packaging layout. Simple, easy, and recyclable packaging not nice seems smooth but additionally reduces waste. Less is regularly greater in this situation.

Tip three: Encourage Recycling.

Include a pleasant word on your package deal encouraging your customers to recycle or reuse the packaging materials. Make them part of the eco-aware movement.

Reducing Shipping Costs and Delivery Times.

Ah, the age-antique struggle: how do you save cash on delivery with out compromising on shipping times? It's a complicated balancing act, but proper right here's how you could hold close it.

Tip 1: Shipping Software.

Invest in transport software. It will let you evaluate expenses from precise companies or perhaps automate a number of your shipping techniques. This saves you time and often coins.

Tip 2: Packaging Efficiency.

Size topics close to packaging. Use containers that are certainly the proper length on your product to keep away from dimensional weight expenses. The smaller, the better.

Tip 3: Negotiate with Carriers.

Don't be afraid to negotiate with your preferred provider. If you are delivery a full-size extent, they'll provide you better fees or reductions. It's well properly well worth a shot!

Use Case: Sara's Sustainable Jewelry Shop.

Take Sara, for example. She runs a a achievement Etsy keep specializing in sustainable rings made from recycled materials. Sara is aware of that her clients are environmentally conscious, so she is going the extra mile collectively along side her shipping and packaging. She makes use of biodegradable bubble wrap, compostable mailers, or maybe consists of a small packet of wildflower seeds in each package deal. Not most effective does this exhibit her determination to sustainability, but it moreover offers a nice contact that her customers adore.

Remember, shipping and packaging are the final steps in the Etsy adventure, but they may be able to leave a long-lasting impact. By deciding on green shipping strategies, inexperienced packaging, and fee-saving strategies, you will no longer most effective pride your customers however furthermore improve your logo's popularity for excellence.

Subsection 4: Dealing with Returns and Refunds.

Ah, the world of e-exchange—the land of opportunity, in which we get to chase our entrepreneurial goals and turn them into truth. But let's accept it; not every sale is rainbows and sunshine. Sometimes, you'll come across a situation wherein a consumer wants to pass returned or exchange a product, or maybe worse, asks for a reimbursement. How you cope with those situations could make or ruin your Etsy keep's recognition. So, permit's dive into the artwork of handling returns and refunds gracefully.

Crafting a Fair and Transparent Return Policy.

Your pass again coverage is the first line of protection on the subject of dealing with returns and refunds. Crafting a clean, honest, and obvious coverage is vital to setting expectations for every you and your customers. Here's the way to transport about it:

1. Be Crystal Clear: Lay out the situations for returns and exchanges in easy language. Specify the time frame inside which returns are giant (e.G., 30 days) and any conditions (e.G., items should be unused and in proper packaging).

2. Spell Out Shipping Costs: Decide whether or now not customers in any other case you, the seller, will endure the go again delivery fees. This is an important element to deal with to avoid disputes later.

3. Offer Options: If possible, provide alternatives for returns and exchanges. Some customers also can select a reimbursement, on the same time as others should probably virtually want a replacement or keep credit score score. Flexibility can pass an extended manner in retaining your customers happy.

four. Honesty Is the Best Policy: If there are gadgets you won't take shipping of returns for (like customized gadgets), make this clean to your coverage. Honesty builds accept as true with.

Handling Returns and Exchanges Smoothly.

Once your flow lower lower back coverage is in place, you may need a systematic approach for handling returns and exchanges. Here's a step-thru-step guide:

1. Communicate Promptly: When a purchaser reaches out approximately a skip lower back or change, reply at once. Courtesy and pace can defuse potentially disturbing conditions.

2. Provide Detailed Instructions: Guide your purchaser thru the method. Explain wherein to supply the object, what facts to embody, and the manner the way works. The extra honest you're making it, the smoother the transaction could be.

3. Inspect Returned Items: Once you get keep of the item, test out it cautiously to make sure

it meets the situations of your go lower back coverage. If it might now not, speak this truly to the patron and supply an cause for why.

4. Process Refunds or Exchanges Quickly: If the object is eligible for a pass lower returned or change, do not drag your ft. Process it rapidly to expose your self-control to amazing customer support.

Issuing Refunds at the same time as Protecting Your Business.

Refunds can be a bitter tablet to swallow, specially if you accept as real with you're within the proper. However, they're on occasion a critical a part of doing industrial organisation. Here's a way to problem them effectively:

1. Stay Professional: No depend variety how nerve-racking the scenario, maintain professionalism in your communications. Avoid getting protective or confrontational.

2. Document Everything: Keep information of all communications and transactions

associated with the refund. This documentation may be useful if a dispute escalates.

3. Know When to Escalate: If a consumer becomes unreasonable or abusive, it is ok to beautify the problem to Etsy's manual group. They can mediate disputes and assist you find out a honest selection.

four. Learn and Improve: After every pass lower back or refund situation, make an effort to reflect. Is there something you may analyze from the revel in to keep away from similar issues within the destiny? Perhaps a product development or clearer communication can prevent destiny disputes.

Remember, even as managing returns and refunds might not be the most glamorous a part of strolling an Etsy keep, it is an essential component of delivering incredible customer service. When handled with equity, transparency, and professionalism, it is able to even beautify your keep's popularity and foster customer loyalty. So, method every go back and refund as an opportunity to expose off your willpower to purchaser pride.

Subsection five: Scaling Customer Loyalty.

Ah, purchaser loyalty — it's the Holy Grail of any a fulfillment organisation. In this monetary disaster, we are going to dive deep into the paintings of turning those one-time customers into devoted enthusiasts who sing your praises from the rooftops. So, capture a cup of your preferred brew, and allow's get started out on building a fan club to your Etsy store.

Implementing a Customer Loyalty Program.

Remember that feeling at the equal time as your chosen espresso preserve surpassed you a loyalty card? It's a warmth, fuzzy feeling, is not it? Well, you could create that equal sentiment to your Etsy hold clients.

Why: A client loyalty software program not simplest incentivizes repeat purchases but additionally fosters a experience of belonging and appreciation among your consumers.

How: Start smooth. Offer a reward for each "x" kind of purchases or a discount on their next order. You also can get revolutionary with special early get proper of get admission to to to new merchandise or participants-handiest profits. Etsy provides reductions, which you could use to reward your reliable shoppers.

Case Study: Sarah's Jewelry Haven achieved a loyalty program presenting a ten% reduce rate on each fifth purchase. Within months, her repeat business organization doubled, and he or she or he decided customers had been looking for extra gadgets to attain that coveted fifth purchase.

Collecting and Utilizing Customer Feedback.

Your customers maintain the important thing for your shop's success, and their comments is like gold. Embrace it, and your save will flourish.

Why: Customer comments enables you recognize what's walking and what goals improvement. It shows your clients that you rate their reviews, which in turn builds don't forget.

How: Start through the use of the usage of soliciting critiques after a buy, and do not be terrified of optimistic complaint. Respond to reviews – each excessive first-rate and awful – professionally and surely. Use surveys to dig deeper into their purchasing for enjoy. Tools like Google Forms or Etsy's non-public survey function can assist.

Case Study: Mary's Handmade Homewares began soliciting for remarks and positioned that her customers loved her merchandise however desired more coloration alternatives. She introduced new sun sun sunglasses, and income skyrocketed.

Turning Satisfied Customers into Brand Advocates.

Your happiest clients are your maximum powerful advertising and marketing device.

They'll shout your praises from the virtual rooftops in case you allow them to.

Why: Word-of-mouth marketing is specially effective, and happy customers are much more likely to refer pals and own family.

How: Encourage happy clients to unfold the phrase. You can offer referral reductions, run contests wherein they percentage their purchases on social media, or maybe create an envoy program to your most devoted enthusiasts.

Case Study: James at CraftyCollectibles have end up his customers into emblem advocates with the resource of website hosting a "Share Your Crafty Corner" contest. Customers published photographs of his merchandise of their homes, and the pleasure on social media brought in new clients by way of way of way of the droves.

Now, it's far your flip to show the ones happy customers into dependable, vocal supporters of your Etsy keep. Remember, constructing consumer loyalty is a journey, no longer a vacation spot. Keep attractive together along with your customers, innovating your loyalty software program, and staying aware about remarks. In doing so, you may create a thriving Etsy empire that now not simplest stands the take a look at of time however additionally leaves a trail of extraordinarily pleased customers in its wake.

Chapter 6: What To Sell

Remember, the whole lot begins collectively alongside your product, so if you've determined to begin an Etsy maintain, the number one trouble to decide is what product you'll promote. This serves as both the muse and the focal point of your preserve.

Alternatively, in all likelihood you're despite the fact that debating a few particular requirements.

For its client base, Etsy offers a massive choice of merchandise for purchase. What are you inclined to promote, but, remains the essential query.

Consider your desires for introduction more carefully proper now. If you recognize, amazing! If now not, don't worry; in truth endure in mind what you're enthusiastic about and notice if that fits.

If you're nonetheless stuck for concept, take a close to take a look at lots of objects and try and recall what it'd take to reveal them into hand-crafted crafts which are unique to you.

Because you enjoy making matters but are stuck for perception, you may have positioned this ebook. In that case, the concept is to select out out what's famous, increase a ultra-contemporary elegance around it, set up a brand, and promote merchandise which are with any luck easy to deliver.

There are severa strategies for figuring out what you want to promote if you are unsure.

Try first surfing some Etsy shops and one-of-a-type online buyers to peer what grabs your interest.

It's crucial to undergo in thoughts what you may purchase.

Your product must be something you care approximately because of the reality you'll be making an investment time in growing it. If you're having problem growing with something, leaf through your personal

Internet browsing records or bear in mind what purchases you've made these days.

You should now have a better idea of the crafts you is probably interested by.

Unfortunately, we're capable of't provide you with a solution to the question of what to sell on Etsy, however with a bit of achievement this text will offer you with a few mind.

An define of a few capability starting elements is supplied under.

Look into any of those that seize your interest.

Investigate the components and time requirements for making them a hint in addition.

Jewelry

One of the most nicely-desired and sought-after gadgets on Etsy proper now is handmade jewelry.

As a end end result, jewelry, necklaces, and bracelets are worn.

These are popular items for clients to shop for both for themselves and as items.

Consider processes to characteristic your private individual and make a chunk of jewellery stand out.

mugs crafted from vinyl.

Unexpectedly many vinyl mugs are available for purchase on Etsy. These mugs are well-known a number of the Etsy community and often characteristic original art work or slogans. This is a brilliant place to start because of the fact you broadly speaking need empty mugs that you may personalize the usage of your personal creativity.

Furthermore, you can settlement out the manufacturing of your vinyl mugs, then promote them for a income.

Toys for kids and infants.

Baby products like headbands and silicone teethers are regularly searched for via Etsy clients.

The name for for one-of-a-kind infant products is also high, which encompass customized storage boxes.

Additionally well-known in recent times are handcrafted timber toys. Look over those and decide which ones, if any, extraordinary wholesome your innovative pressure.

stickers and planners.

The stage of name for for planners and stickers on Etsy can also wonder you.

Calendars and stickers are possible giveaways.

Although the get right of entry to barrier is pretty low, printing fees and other charges ought to be taken beneath consideration.

Products for pets.

It isn't always any wonder that pup-associated gadgets do nicely on Etsy due to the truth human beings inside the US, Canada, Europe, and first-rate factors of the arena adore their pets. The merchandise for dogs and cats may be the most famous.

For an awful lot much less fashionable pets like snakes, lizards, and ferrets, you can additionally discover a niche market.

In this magnificence, there are numerous alternatives for collars, bowls, toys, and some detail else that puppy owners may additionally want.

Additionally, you'll be capable of promote extra pup merchandise in case you customize them.

Tools and patterns for sewing.

Some of the maximum famous Etsy stores promote sewing materials like zippers, fabric swatches, embroidered patches, and zips.

There is usually a advantage in now not having to make these objects yourself.

Another developing style is using stitching patterns.

If you regularly stitch and experience growing via, this is a notable desire.

It may not be appropriate for you if no longer.

Self-Care Items.

On Etsy, call for for self-care products is continuously excessive. This includes lip balms, artisan soaps, massage oils, and tub and body products.

You could be nicely on your way to amazing success if you manage to discover a wholesale company with high-quality objects.

Finding a way to personalize those devices so they end up precise expressions of you is the hard part.

Cases for cellular devices.

It's no longer surprising that there's a massive demand for cell cellphone instances on Etsy.

Many humans invest in enhancing the aesthetics of their present day-day cell phones. Cases that appearance pinnacle and defend the telephone nicely will normally be popular.

Products for weddings.

For their specific day, people want some component virtually one-of-a-type at weddings and anniversaries.

Depending on what you want to make, this could encompass a extensive kind of crafts.

Handmade corsages, decorations, décor, and invitations are a number of the often sold wedding ceremony items.

GIVING THOUGHT TO YOUR PRODUCT.

It's time to offer it a few notion now that we've discussed a few thoughts.

Consider the subsequent whilst you don't forget you could understand what you need to sell.

Are you glad developing it?

It's critical to be honest with yourself because of the truth you may't faux to experience the method.

In order on your creativity to go back via, you want to pick a product that you in reality revel in growing.

Even worse, in case you dislike making it, you'll probably begin to dislike it.

Is it famous?

Since developments can trade short, offering a way to this question can be hard.

You also can ask your self, "Will there be an target marketplace that goals my product?" Even notwithstanding the truth that you don't have the maximum famous products within the marketplace, you need to have as a minimum some potential customers. If you discover that simplest a small amount of people are interested by your concept, don't forget expanding it.

Consider making collars for extraordinary animals if, as an instance, you're making ferret collars.

Does your product present room for boom?

A more tough question, but one that merits hobby however.

The greater procedures you could provide version to customers, the better. If you're making craft additives, can you change the colors?

If you need to promote a few kind of apparel, can you convert the pattern or the format?

How masses attempt is going into producing your gadgets?

When locating out which product to sell, that is one of the maximum large factors which you'll want to recall.

We advocate reading approximately the strategies involved in producing pretty a few gadgets to determine which might be possible.

You need to keep in mind some things, which includes:.

how an lousy lot time the manner desires.

how difficult it is.?

what additives you require.?

The time it takes to make a product can range, but you need to pay close to hobby to the substances which can be desired.

It's crucial to be aware of whether the substances required for a craft are available everywhere you are.

You should moreover check to see if they are provided at an low-priced price if they're.

Here, searching at the materials is a essential step. You need to deliver this cautious concept due to the fact you could stumble upon troubles if the materials required to make a few detail are not effectively to be had or are too difficult to acquire.

AN EXAMPLE OF PRODUCT CREATION.

You should be considering your craft's materials and manufacturing system via this factor. You might also want to reconsider your alternatives if neither of these works out for you. Let's take a look at an instance so you can see what this shows greater without a doubt. We'll observe the stairs involved in making candles. That applies to each the substances and the actual steps involved in developing a candle. Only 9 pretty honest steps make up the whole method. Similar to developing a batch, it doesn't soak up an entire lot of time—approximately an hour. Moreover, the amount of materials you require. Virtually falls pretty low.

You must now have a better statistics of processes candles are made no matter the reality that each one of these examples were pretty simplified.

Candlemaking Materials.

Wax.

Wicks.

Candle containers (glasses,tins,jars, and so forth.). Boiling pot.

tape used for protecting.

Scale.

Thermometer.

Whatever scents you need to encompass.

Simple Steps for Making Candles.

Wax is measured.

Burnish the wax.

Fancy oils can be delivered.

Put the candle containers collectively.

Add the wick.

Wax is poured.

Fix the wick.

Refill the wax.

Trim the wick.

It's exceptional if you're getting thoughts from the ones nine steps, however try to maintain in mind that that is first-class the general layout of a recipe. In fact, every craft, which encompass candles, wishes some element remarkable to set it aside.

Even although the aforementioned system need to excellent take approximately an hour, you'll though need to test plenty to offer the final product that you need to provide to clients. When measuring out the wax, as an instance, at step one, your cease cause will assist you decide the right quantity. The 1/3 step, in which the oils are added, is the equal. There is a wealth of information available on line approximately the kinds, quantities, and combos of vital oils to apply.

But in the long run, you're going to have to test for some time before you find out the best recipe.

RESEARCH IS KEY.

When you have a selected craft in mind which you want to sell, now could be the time to investigate more about it. Learn all you may about it. Take into attention the following:.

How is it created?

Can it is made at domestic?

What unique device will you require?

How prolonged does it take to make?

What sources will it require to be made?

Who makes purchases of this object?

The product is the muse of your Etsy store, as we formerly said, so you must be wonderful of the whole lot earlier than growing a desire.

Make a few more inquiries to yourself.

The motive of this exercising is to decide whether or no longer or no longer you're more professional than your opposition, whether or not or no longer your closest rival is lots of miles away, and whether or now not or now not there are sufficient products in the marketplace to meet all needs.

Determine who will buy it in addition to whether or no longer you may sell. This brings up the subsequent mission.

Who Is Your Target Market?

You cannot surely positioned your product handy and count on to peer results right away, there can be no question about that.

You need to go through in thoughts the people who might be intrigued sufficient thru way of your product to make a purchase, to put it as truly as feasible.

The notable way to determine what you need to perform is to bear in thoughts it out of your private thoughts-set.

You can collect a latest profile of your functionality customers via responding to the subsequent questions: What piqued your hobby in the product; what influenced you to do that; who turn out to be the primary to buy it on the equal time as you first presented it; do you remember you studied this product is attractive to you; might you buy this product if it have been made to be had to you. Then, the usage of your observations and the people who've been identified as customers of your rival's merchandise which can be much like yours, you could study greater and enlarge your goal marketplace even extra.

If there can be very little hobby to your product, it's miles possible that humans are unaware of it. You can open your keep if your studies indicates that there may be a enough quantity of hobby in what you want to offer.

Always search for comparable merchandise as properly. Consider whether or not comparable merchandise are being sold. If you're making some trouble one-of-a-kind, the solution to the query "Is your product particular in a specific manner?" is plain.

There isn't any one to mission you. It's time to endure in mind why customers might select out your products over those of your combatants in case you are generating handcrafted gadgets which may be identical to or similar to those bought with the aid of manner of using others.

Examine the inclinations.

Once you have an idea, you may need to have a observe inclinations to appearance what a tremendous place to begin is probably. For this, the style show on Etsy is an internet net page for trending products that can be beneficial.

You can see what humans are looking for on web sites like Twitter, Buzzfeed, and Google. It may be brilliant in case you enabled notifications for this and monitored some social media.

In addition to subscribing to 3 web websites and periodicals related to crafts and layout, you need to hold an eye fixed fixed fixed out for what's trending on Pinterest, Amazon, and eBay.

Don't just follow the institution, however additionally don't look ahead to whatever to emerge as old. Moving from one concept to every extraordinary can be excellent quite regularly.

Are mini letters being made that you may ship in your friends? What amazing tiny things can also want to you are making?

A specific aspect.

Once you've finished your studies and recognized a product that looks promising, discover a manner to transform that craft into some component this is truly unique.

Being in a position to shop for some thing particular, one-of-a-kind, or personalized is one of the fundamental attracts on Etsy. As a end result, having a crafted from the very exceptional caliber or one this is really unique is not always vital. Giving it a unique feeling is the important thing.

Chapter 7: Setting Up Your Shop

It's time to open your keep when you've determined on your product. This is a vital step because of the reality customers' first impressions of your product is probably shaped with the useful resource of your Etsy preserve. You need to pay near interest.

The way you gift your product is a crucial detail of the patron's normal enjoy together together with your keep and brand, and we're right proper right here due to the fact every detail counts. The presentation's relaxation, which culminates in the consumer's hands-on enjoy with the product, is ready in movement with the resource of the client's initial view of a product picture.

In Chapter 1, we mentioned a manner to set up your maintain, but now allow's delve a little deeper.

It's important to list your product with descriptive and appealing snap shots in case you need to attract in clients who are keen to shop for what you're imparting.

Here, permit's pass over some of the essential steps.

Establish a profile.

Choose a store call.

Describe your product.

Take pics of your products.

developing product descriptions.

Take gain of seo.

choosing a name on your e-alternate preserve.

The first step after developing your Etsy account is choosing a company.

Being capable of change your call after selecting it makes this a tough challenge. Let's talk what a name on Etsy approach now.

choosing a call.

It's crucial to offer cautious attention on your preserve's or preserve's call. Having a call that humans do not forget should make or harm your organisation agency because of the fact first impressions are so essential.

Depending in your store's call, customers may additionally decide to visit or skip it with the useful resource of.

In slight of this, you need to choose out out a name a terrific way to will let you appeal to inside the most clients.

Always hold in thoughts that the decision is essential for recognition via the target market, fashion, and searchability. Here are a few recommendations to help you in choosing an appropriate name to your store.

As an awful lot as you could, mirror the product you're selling.

If you need to make it easier for human beings to discover your industrial agency, you could pick out a call that consists of the fine gadgets you're promoting.

Make fantastic your save call consists of the phrase "coaster" in case you sell customized coasters, as an instance.

Customers searching out coasters can be drawn for your save as rapid as they see the call and will input.

Additionally, naming your product topics helps with seo, developing the hazard that functionality customers will locate your product once they behavior a look for it.

However, there may be a disadvantage to doing so. If you decide to extend your product services, it might be tough to draw clients, in particular in the occasion that they already partner your hold with coasters.

Be privy to your spelling.

A call that is easy to mention and spell is some thing you want to aim for. While it is pretty recommended which you come up with a completely unique and outstanding name, you want to try to keep away from making topics tough in your clients by means of the usage of manner of the use of atypical or unusual terms.

Before choosing a name with specific characters, you want to additionally make sure. Your aim must be to use famous terminology and correct spelling due to the truth doing it this manner will make it much less complex for functionality clients to don't forget and sort the decision of your save into the search bar.

If you choose a name this is hard to spell, customers also can type it incorrectly and be directed to each different shop. You run the chance of dropping customers whilst this takes place. You are well conscious that having fewer customers will harm the fulfillment of your employer.

Be concise and straightforward.

As an entire lot as you can, you want to avoid giving your save a prolonged call. It takes a whole lot of time to kind and is tough to bear in mind. As a end stop end result, you have to take some time to preserve the decision of your hold straightforward and concise.

It isn't endorsed to use extra than three terms.

Test your reminiscence thru taking the exercising.

You aren't required to take this test in a checking out facility. You can complete it at your very personal pace and inside the convenience of your property. Truth be knowledgeable, it's quite easy.

Try to don't forget which Etsy shops stuck your interest on the same time as you have got were given a pen and paper close by.

List the names of those stores. Whether you want the products offered in that maintain or no longer is beside the factor. Now all you want to do is jot down the names of the shops that pop into your head.

Once you're completed, appearance over those names all once more to look if there may be a few detail you could discover in commonplace with them. Take under consideration what makes.

they'll be ear-catching and tremendous. Use them as a start line for your preserve's name after that.

To discover what you're looking for, use search engines like google

Try searching for the object you preference to promote the usage of any search engine you could recollect, which encompass Google, Bing, or Yahoo.

After getting into your preferred name, test out the number one net page of consequences.

It might not be a great idea to pick out a call if the search already returns quite some shops, blogs, or web sites with a comparable call because it might be extra hard to distinguish your emblem.

Avoid relating to humans in a derogatory manner.

On Etsy, it's miles forbidden to use terms which may be considered vulgar or offensive. Therefore, when selecting phrases, you need to maintain with the maximum care. Make sure you choose the appropriate name for your first attempt because of the truth starting a new corporation definitely based totally on its name may be tough and stressful.

It additionally can be hard to attract clients in your new maintain when you have already constructed a following below your previous name as it is probably taxing so one can pass your property.

Even worse, you obtained't be capable of switch any of your previous income data, conversations, feedback, or different interactions for your new store.

Verify that the selected call is not already in use.

Getting sued over the name of your Etsy preserve is simply not what you want. Therefore, ensure to stick to neighborhood, kingdom, and/or national jail pointers earlier than choosing the selection of your save.

The reality that a few names and phrases have already been registered as logos want to be saved in thoughts.

They can't be used as a end result.

You can find out if a name has already been registered via getting into touch together together with your Secretary of State.

Additionally, you could visit the united states Patent and Trademark Office internet web page.

You can also ask a specialist for crook recommendation.

Allow your area of understanding and enjoy of style to come lower back thru.

Pick a call for your company that captures each the personality of the owner and the cultured of the goods.

For instance, you want to offer you with a name that is right for the gadgets you're selling if they are a laugh and unusual.

If you are marketing traditional objects, pick out a name this is attractive or stylish.

Do now not be afraid to apply all your innovative creativeness at the same time as developing with a call on your maintain. After all, you need humans to accomplice you and your merchandise at the side of your keep.

A LISTING OF YOUR GOOD.

How to Take Successful Pictures.

When it involves promoting on Etsy or everywhere else, pictures are essential.

You want to offer outstanding visual aids because you lack a bodily vicinity in which your customers can browse your products.

Even although pictures can't quite observe to the real factor, they nevertheless give the viewer an amazing concept and a long-lasting impact.

Consequently, you need to take all affordable steps to ensure that the pics you upload are of the remarkable super.

Your These pics need to permit capability customers to get a enjoy of approaches your products sense and appear.

Listed underneath are a few hints for including snap shots in your Etsy store:.

Invest in a digicam with a excessive decision.

To ensure the fine viable high-quality of your photographs, you need to use a tremendous digital camera as a notable deal as you could.

A big preference of digital cameras are to be had in case you need to select out from.

Always have a look at opinions and evaluation the specs in advance than creating a final buy.

If you cannot come up with the money for a greater expensive one, you could use your telephone. Do not be involved; there are strategies you may use to beautify your pix even in case you quality used your smartphone.

Later on in this book, the ones techniques may be blanketed in more detail.

Use the macro settings in your digital digital camera to take near-up pix.

The incredible majority of devices supplied at the net web page are compact sufficient to be used in a macro surroundings.

This putting is regularly represented by way of a flower or tulip icon.

On the possibility hand, you are not required to paste to a unmarried putting.

You are welcome to check with numerous settings to determine which one great fits you.

Try out numerous pairings to look which one works best.

Don't use your flash digital digital camera.

Some business enterprise owners make the error of taking images with flash system.

Compare the snap shots you took with and without the flash on your virtual digital camera, listening to the variations.

you'll do.

observe that photographs focused on out a flash seem plenty higher.

This is because of the flash's light output, which skews the picture because it displays off the state of affairs.

If you need your pics to appear brighter, skip someplace where the lighting fixtures is brilliant however diffused.

For taking pix outdoor, the lights is proper because of the fact it's miles brilliant and natural.

Use herbal mild instead of synthetic lighting.

Outside, there's first rate lighting for taking pix.

However, it isn't counseled to stand within the direct sunlight hours.

Your snap shots will lose top notch as a surrender quit result.

Instead, use oblique moderate to take the snap shots.

Put your self in a shaded area or somewhere that is not proper now in the sun.

For example, you could maintain to use the patio.

Take advantage of numerous props.

Including props along aspect your merchandise can produce beautiful photos.

Props are to be had for buy from region of know-how stores or may be created at home with objects you have already got to be had. Flowers, as an instance, may be used to decorate the enchantment and class of your merchandise.

A toddler's outfit can be complemented via small toys.

Balloons, books, and other appropriate devices additionally can be used to beautify the photographs.

For example, herbs are exquisite elaborations for home made shampoo and cleansing cleansing cleaning soap.

Additionally, hats and one of a kind garb objects can be displayed the usage of a model.

The item can be modeled on your body in case you don't have any props.

An apron would possibly appearance higher on you on a strong color historic past than a stable colour information.

It may be greater attractive to tie a scarf spherical your neck than to certainly lie on the ground.

Potential customers can see how your products will seem in person with the aid of manner of sporting samples of them.

existence. On the opportunity hand, be cautious for going too far.

Keep in mind that the priority of the picture want to be the number one attention, now not the props. Even in case you use attractive props, your items need to command hobby.

Make your item stand out with the resource of selecting a heritage that does so.

In photos, backgrounds are essential.

If you don't have any matching props, you can use backgrounds with prints or patterns.

A distracting historical past ought to be averted, despite the fact that.

An unadorned historical past is every specific opportunity. Any robust coloration will do, however the satisfactory selections are white and black.

With the exception of white merchandise, nearly some thing seems accurate in competition to a white records.

On the alternative hand, black backgrounds beautify the appearance of items that are white, gold, silver, or neon-colored.

In this situation, contrast is vital, so maintain that during mind. When using mild or pastel-coloured devices, you ought to choose a historic past that is darker.

On the other hand, in case your items are darkish in color, you want to apply a lighter statistics.

Take snap shots from numerous angles.

To permit your clients to look how your product seems from the front, again, factors, top, and bottom, make sure to take numerous pix of it.

Select the high-quality snap shots from every viewpoint after taking some pics from each attitude.

Make superb to embody all the important pictures while you bear in mind that Etsy allows sellers to feature as tons as 5 photos in line with listing.

Include a photo that shows one-of-a-kind angles from which your item can be seen.

Be powerful to consist of every close to-up and large-scale snap shots.

your acquiescence.

This will permit clients to view every detail of the product.

To decorate your pics, use a photo editor.

Editing refers to improving in region of clearly changing something's appearance. Don't mislead your functionality clients thru making your merchandise seem like a few component they are now not with the resource of changing the way it appears inside the pix, which want to nonetheless display your item.

After taking the image, add it to a picture editor to decorate the great.

When looking to make pics seem to had been taken by way of a professional photographer, photo editors are beneficial.

Two examples of what you could do are to exchange the contrast and decrease the ancient past noise.

To defend your photographs, you could furthermore use a copyright watermark.

You may be tremendous that nobody else will take your images and use them for his or her very non-public benefit on this way. However, so long as they broadly recognized and request your permission first, you could though permit others to use your photos, likely as a deliver of belief.

In the section that follows, we'll speak extra approximately photo improving.

Describe the scenario.

It can be tough for capability customers to decide an item's length even as it stands on my own in a photo.

You need to therefore supply your clients a revel in of scale.

By taking pix of your devices with both you or a model, you could gather this. It may also be located on show next to a cherished animal or particular recognizable item.

For example, if you promote handcrafted dolls, your customers won't understand how huge or small they'll be until you placed them subsequent to something.

already are privy to its size.

The doll can consequently be photographed while being propped up to your palm if it's far only the size of your palm and you are selling it.

This may additionally want to supply your clients a higher impression of the manner big it's far instead of honestly laying it down at the ground and taking a photograph.

You can cling an artwork up in your wall and take photos of it in case you're promoting it.

If you're promoting rings, you may do considered certainly one of subjects: keep it up or placed on it.

To show it, you could additionally use a version.

In relation to apparel, the identical is proper. The clothing may be worn by way of way of the use of you or located on a life-duration version.

Writing Powerful Descriptions.

A nicely product description is vital for attractive customers and helping them take a look at extra about your merchandise.

They is probably more inclined to make a purchase as a surrender end result. The right artwork can convince capacity clients to feature your merchandise to their buying carts.

You could likely discover that writing your product descriptions is tough if you are new to Etsy. However, with a few exercising, you'll be able to create splendid product descriptions speedy.

To be triumphant as a dealer at the internet site, maintain in thoughts the following present day guidelines.

Avoid burying the lede.

Visitors ought to examine your description and recognition on the most important facts about your product.

This gives brief get admission to to information approximately your product for capability clients.

In addition to offering juicy facts thru it, you can optimize how this description appears inside the are searching for results.

Don't worry; you can but use terms from the pick out of your item.

Personalize the whole lot.

Even despite the fact that people generally want to interact with others on a more private stage, you first-class have a lot time to have interaction a capacity patron. Consider writing inside the first man or woman; it will assist you to hook up with readers in my opinion and is a rather effective method.

You ought to therefore show some individual in your clients in preference to without a doubt being a faceless salesclerk.

Like a primary meeting with a new acquaintance, think about your product descriptions as such.

You need to come upon as excellent at the identical time as notwithstanding the truth that acting natural.

To make your writing easy to examine, use bullet factors and brief paragraphs.

You should be conscious that some customers who visit your keep are searching for a specific fabric or duration.

Use bullet points and brief paragraphs to set up and make vital data greater seen for them to apprehend.

Do now not use terms which can be useless or illogical.

The message you are trying to keep to potential clients ought to be concise and easy.

In this way, your hyperlinks can direct functionality customers to at least one-of-a-kind components or sections of your shop wherein they could analyze more approximately you and your merchandise if your product description isn't always convincing enough to steer them. They may be directed to your About Page, in which they may look at approximately your private success story, aspirations, and desires in your keep.

After locating out extra about you and your organisation and establishing a non-public connection, ability customers might be persuaded to transact company with you.

Make an attempt to find your non-public voice.

Remember that the tone of your writing will determine the precise fashion or character of your keep.

Keep your meant purpose marketplace in thoughts at the same time as developing your voice.

Think approximately the message you want to bring to them. If the majority of your clients are women searching out presents for his or her boyfriends or husbands, or men who're engaged and approximately to get married, you can modify your product listings to meet their desires.

There are a whole lot of products that can be offered, which includes men's apparel, watches, fragrance, and different non-public objects.

Questions Your Etsy Descriptions Should Be Able to Answer.

In addition to the aforementioned advice, you ought if you need to reply to the most preferred purchaser problems and troubles with answers and answers.

Remember that the majority of those one-time customers won't be able to address, sense, scent, or attempt to your products.

Because of this, you ought to provide them the information they need as when you have been their eyes, ears, nose, and pores and pores and skin.

Potential customers are more likely to click on on on "upload to basket" than "decrease returned" and in no manner come lower once more in your keep if the product descriptions pique their interest.

Or to place it each distinctive way, a sale will best achieve success if your product descriptions are correct.

Here are a few of the maximum preferred client queries which you want to be equipped to answer in order that will help you.

What separates and distinguishes your products?

Your product descriptions want to consist of a few element, ideally a narrative. This tale ought to be compelling sufficient to persuade others to shop for from you and visit your save all another time within the destiny.

But it isn't always essential to have a lengthy story. However, it wants to be prolonged enough for a capability purchaser of your items to emerge as acquainted with you.

Consider the advertisements for soda.

Since advertising and marketing is extra regularly than now not about selling a sensation or a want, it's not going which you've ever seen a well-known logo's component-focused industrial.

Relationship constructing alongside aspect your customers is critical.

Consequently, you are passing up a huge threat to make an affect and win over capacity clients in case you high-quality use a product description to highlight the physical tendencies of your devices.

What gadgets them other than merchandise which are similar to them?

Although Etsy merchandise are hand made, unique, and not heavily produced in a manufacturing unit, there may be a opportunity that there are other devices like yours on the internet site.

There's an extremely good threat that precise people make and sell comparable merchandise besides you. If you promote knitwear, for example, you have to count on that particular carriers will do the equal.

Since knitted sweaters and different items of garb are quite common, you'll need to make certain yours stands proud.

So, one way to differentiate your objects is to demonstrate and justify how they have got a aggressive facet. Make sure to emphasize the particular factors of your products at the equal time as closing, and describe what makes them stand proud of those of your opposition.

being considerate of various sellers.

You can also speak about how your merchandise may make your clients' lives extra accessible, fun, or easy.

What devices your products aside?

Your product descriptions need to consist of some detail, preferably a tale. This tale need to be convincing enough to bring about others to shop for a few component and are to be had returned for your hold in a while.

A brief story like this may be informed, despite the fact that. However, it want to ultimate extended sufficient for a potential purchaser of your products to grow to be familiar with you.

Consider the commercials for soda.

Since advertising and marketing is specifically about promoting an emotion or a choice, it's not going which you've ever visible an industrial for a well-known logo that specializes inside the materials.

It's crucial to assemble a courting collectively with your clients.

Consequently, you are passing up a huge chance to make a power and win over ability customers in case you high-quality use a product description to spotlight the bodily developments of your gadgets.

What sets them apart from competing merchandise which can be similar to them?

Even though Etsy merchandise are hand made, particular, and now not intently produced in a production unit, there may be a threat that there are precise devices like yours at the internet net web page.

There's a exquisite chance that exclusive people make and sell comparable merchandise except you. If you promote knitwear, for instance, you want to anticipate that exceptional vendors will do the identical.

You want to make your knitted item stand out due to the fact that knitted sweaters and different clothing are quite not unusual. So, how do you differentiate your gadgets from the opposition?

One manner is to illustrate and justify how they have a competitive part.

Make sure to emphasize the only of a kind capabilities of your merchandise on the equal time as final, and describe what makes them stand pleased with the ones of your competitors.

regard for unique dealers.

You can also provide an reason in the back of how your merchandise might in all likelihood beautify the satisfactory, comfort, or ease of your clients' lives.

How many products are there in overall?

The quantity is generally apparent.

On the opportunity hand, a few might require an extensive clarification.

When a purchaser will pay in your product, you have to specify what number of quantities they'll get keep of.

Greeting cards and craft substances often display off this.

All stationery is inside the identical boat, which includes domestic made envelopes.

Is the dimensions of your buy first-rate for you?

For gadgets which might be supposed to be worn, that is in particular critical.

For shirts, blouses, slacks, skirts, and some thing else someone would possibly placed on, measurements should be taken.

Socks, hats, and other accessories can be photographed on a version or model.

You need to positioned the items on a model or mannequin in order to reveal them at a scale.

If not, it might be difficult to inform whether or not or no longer or no longer they may be too small or massive for the wearer. The principal objective is to demonstrate to clients how the object will appear on them.

What does the element do?

Always bear in thoughts to consist of one or "movement shots.". These present your product in its appropriate setting. This is especially true if your products are supposed to be used in combination with specific topics.

You must display your product protective an iPad if you are promoting an iPad stand, as an instance.

You have to use a smartphone to illustrate a mobile smartphone case in case you are selling one. You should private a valid passport that bears the image of the passport holder.

if you market custom passport covers.

Let's say you're a dealer of downloadable recipe books; what if your product is a few component that can be downloaded?

By creating a dish and putting the recipe next to it, you may display your recipe to functionality clients. This will supply ability clients an idea of the manner the dish will flip out and what to expect after they purchase and down load your online recipe e-book.

What additives do your merchandise consist of?

It is essential to permit your customers understand what substances went into making your products.

www.ingramcontent.com/pod-product-compliance
Lightning Source LLC
Chambersburg PA
CBHW071441080526
44587CB00014B/1939